Lyric Poets of the Southern T'ang

Daniel Bryant

Lyric Poets of The Southern T'ang

Feng Yen-ssu, 903–960, and Li Yü, 937–978

UNIVERSITY OF BRITISH COLUMBIA PRESS
VANCOUVER AND LONDON

LYRIC POETS OF THE SOUTHERN T'ANG
FENG YEN-SSU, 903–960, AND LI YÜ, 937–978

This book has been published with the help of a grant
from the Canadian Federation for the Humanities, using
funds provided by the Social Sciences and Humanities Research
Council of Canada.

Canadian Cataloguing in Publication Data

Main entry under title:
Lyric poets of the southern T'ang

Includes selections from Yang ch'un chi, by Feng Yen-ssu, and the text of Nan T'ang erh chu tz'u, by Li Yü and Li Ching.
Bibliography: p.
ISBN 0-7748-0142-5

1. Tz'u—Translations into English. 2. English poetry—Translations from Chinese. I. Bryant, Daniel Joseph, 1942–II. Feng, Yen-ssu, 903–960. Yang ch'un chi. III. Li, Yü, 937–978. Nan T'ang erh chu tz'u. IV. Li, Ching, 916–961.

PL2658.E3L96   895.1'1'308   C82-091110-0

ISBN-0-7748-0142-5

Printed in Canada

in memory of
Sharon Klein
and
Henry W. Wells

CONTENTS

PREFACE

This book, small as it is, has been a long time in the making. In 1966, not long after I first began the study of Chinese, I began to wish for something "real" to practise on. With this in mind, I saved up a sum equivalent to a week's wages and sent it off to a reputable book dealer in Hong Kong, from whom, not long after, I began to receive box after box of Chinese books, including most of the Confucian Classics, the early philosophers, several historical works, and a great variety of poetry, fiction, and drama. I was then in something of a predicament, for I was still painfully deciphering even very simple materials at the rate of a few lines a day, and it looked as though I now had a library that I should be several lifetimes in reading. Clearly, if great discouragement were to be avoided, I should have to make a choice from my trove and do so with some care. Sorting through the lot—many of the titles were still unknown to me— I came to what was clearly the slimmest volume, "The Lyric Poems of Li Yü" (*Li Hou-chu Tz'u*). I set to work on this, and by the time I returned to University three years later I had accumulated draft translations of most of the poems. In my graduating year at the University of British Columbia, I chose Li Yü as the topic of my honours essay. I had already begun to translate Feng Yen-ssu as well and continued to work on both poets at intervals during my graduate work in Vancouver and Kyōto. Once I had finished my dissertation, on an unrelated topic, late in 1977, I returned to Feng and Li and, with further delays occasioned by teaching duties and other projects, completed the bulk of the present work during the next two years, though in revising it just prior to publication I have tried to incorporate references to significant research published up to about the end of 1980.

My main aim in preparing this book has been to make available to Western readers a significant body of translations from this important and rewarding part of China's literary heritage. But it seemed a good idea to provide the poems with an introductory essay discussing their historical and literary context as well. In this essay I have tried to take into account all the directly relevant secondary literature, though my conclusions in some cases differ from those hitherto current. For example, I have tried to place Li Yü, an immensely popular poet sometimes treated as though he were a happy accident, in a more realistic perspective by giving roughly equal space to his near contemporary Feng Yen-ssu, who (it seems to me) is generally under-valued. I have also tried to concentrate on the poems of both men rather than on their lives, though the latter were so interesting that they have occasionally intruded themselves in spite of my efforts. I have devoted a good deal of attention to the poetic form in which most of the works of both poets are cast, the *tz'u*. In this my attention has been directed more at the generic characteristics of the *tz'u* than at its historical development up to the time of the Southern T'ang poets. I do sketch the latter briefly, but for a more detailed account in English, the interested reader is directed to an excellent study published since I completed the drafting of this book, Kang-i Sun Chang's *The Evolution of Chinese* Tz'u *Poetry*. I have not discussed textual problems here, not because I think the textual history of the poems uncomplicated or unimportant, but rather because it is so complicated and I think it so important that I am treating it in several specialized articles variously in press or in preparation. My present judgments in matters textual are implicit in the translations.

The world of sinology is currently in the midst of a heated methodological debate over the translation of Chinese poetry, and I should say something in defence of the approach that I have adopted. I have tried to steer a middle course between, on the one hand, the impressionistic and often solecism-ridden daydreams of the pick-and-choose faction, which holds that a line of Chinese verse can be construed in all manner of ways and that a translator is free to "plunk down" for the one he likes best, and, on the other, the excessive and often simply fussy rigidity of the "always and indubitably" school, which believes that Chinese poetry has a regular and unvarying syntax whose workings must be exactly reproduced in English along with the precise lexical meaning of each word. The latter group is, I believe, generally right about Chinese, and their commitment to accurate understanding is a worthy cause. But they are often wrong about English, or at least insensitive to it, tending to produce ponies laden with neologisms unintelligible to all but those able to read the original texts. Although the syntax of Chinese is in many respects much more like that of English than is the case with Latin or Japanese—the difficulties inherent in the literalist approach would be exposed at once were its principles applied to Ovid or Issa—it does do some things that simply have no equivalent in idiomatic English, and I see no advantage for either philology or literature in translating grace by awkwardness where it can be avoided. With one or two exceptions, the translations in this volume are intended to be renderings as faithful to the sense and syntax of their originals as is consistent with the translation of their single most important "meaning," that they are poetry. Colour words in particular have been rendered according to context. Thus I have translated the troublesome word *ts'ui*, literally "halcyon king-fisher," as "raven" in Feng Yen-ssu's poem LIII and elsewhere not through ignorance of ornithology, but rather because "raven" is the word we use in English to indicate the iridescent sheen of black hair and similar effects. In the same way, the "black birds" of Feng's poem VII and elsewhere are actually *ch'ing-niao* in the original, *ch'ing* being a dark natural colour, most commonly blue or green, but occasionally grey or black. Here it seemed as important to avoid the associations of "bluebirds" in English as to render the colour word consistently (and in fact the anecdote to which the poems allude specifies "black"). Such are the trials of genuine translation, which, like politics, is an art of the possible. Doubters are urged to reread the eminently sensible remarks of Professor Owen in the July 1979 issue of *Chinese Literature, Essays, Articles, Reviews* and to seek for dictionary equivalents in dictionaries. Meaning aside, I have attempted to reproduce something of the metrical pattern of the poems by matching the number of stressed syllables in each line of the translations to the number of syllables in the original. Where this proved too difficult, I have tried to shorten or extend lines of corresponding length equally, but in a few cases even this compromise was impossible.

A word needs to be added concerning the presence of a phonetic transcription of the poems. Such transcriptions are frequently included with translations of Japanese verse, but not often with Chinese, perhaps because it is felt—with some justification—that even modern Chinese is a much more difficult language for an English speaker to pronounce. All the same, since these poems were originally intended for vocal performance, one would seem to owe any venturesome readers a chance to attempt a recitation for themselves. Moreover, the phonetic patterns revealed by the transcription are an integral part of the structure of the poems, for they enrich the significance of each by underlining or subverting its semantic structure, accelerating or retarding the metre, and so forth. Both of these considerations require, of course, that the transcription reflect the pronunciation of Southern T'ang Chinese, not present-day Mandarin, a language in many respects remarkably unlike that of the tenth century. Indeed, to recite these poems in Mandarin, as is commonly done today, tells us no more about their original phonetic qualities than a Brazilian priest's chanting of the Latin Mass tells us about the prosody of Catullus. The system used for the transcription is explained, with a pronunciation guide, at the end of the introduction. Although its general outlines are quite reliable, there are numerous points of detail over which specialists continue to disagree. Moreover, there are some characters for which early sources give multiple pronunciations, and it is sometimes difficult to decide between these. I have cut through all the Gordian knots with a variety of blades, and if some of these should prove to have been duller than others, I hope that the rough edges will be forgiven. In any event, it is essential that we become more conscious of the sound of early Chinese poetry, especially the *tz'u*, and it seemed better to begin responding to this need than to hold back for fear of making mistakes in matters of detail.

So far as other conventions are concerned, I have transcribed Chinese terms according to the Wade-Giles system, still the standard for serious writing on Chinese subjects, except that I follow James J. Y. Liu and others in consistently using the syllable *yi* for the two equivalent forms *yi* and *i*. I have also differed from common practice in the capitalization of Chinese and Japanese titles, treating them as intelligible labels rather than as strings of nonsense syllables.

The faith of anyone who still believes that virtue and generosity have their recognition and reward in this world will be sorely tried by the reflection that no one has yet published a first book on a Chinese subject whose acknowledgement section exceeded its text in length—as it ought. I shall not stray from what is conventional in this, even at the cost of doing injustice, but at least some of the help I have received must be acknowledged here. My very first Chinese teacher at Berkeley, Clarence Shangraw, now at the Brundage Collection, put up with a great deal of nonsense and truancy from me, never failing to respond with patient encouragement. After I left Berkeley, it was that encouragement (along with a passing mark that I had not yet earned) and the intellectual examples of David Lewin and the late Joseph Levenson and Seymour Shifrin that kept me at it. At McGill, at the time of my earliest struggles with the translation of these poems, David L. Kuan kindly read a draft paper including about two dozen of them. A little later, Chang Hui-mei, now Jennie Chang Orlov, patiently devoted hours to answering my queries. I am also grateful to my friends Charles and Vicky Palmer, now of Antigonish, Nova Scotia, for the summers I spent on their farm in Havelock, Quebec, as *homme engagé* and translator-in-residence. It was on one of my solitary evening walks there that the present book first took shape in my mind. At the University of British Columbia, Yeh Chia-ying (Florence C. Y. Chao) and Jan W. Walls gave generously of their time and erudition as advisors to my honours essay. Mr. Shui-yim Tse of the University Library introduced me to research materials and methodologies with a thoroughness from which I am still profiting. Also in Vancouver, E. G. Pulleyblank initiated me into the mysteries of historical phonology and eventually succeeded in making them less mysterious. He has subsequently put me in his debt by his acute criticism of my attempts, here and elsewhere, to apply what I had learned from him to the study of literature. In Kyōto, Lai Wood-yan, now of the University of Hong Kong, was of great help in our many friendly discussions of Chinese literature, and of Li Yü in particular. More recently, Jan Walls, now a colleague in Victoria, and Kang-i Sun Chang have given the introduction the benefit of their critical readings. My friends Ray and Pat Young have greatly facilitated my work by their hospitality during my research trips to Vancouver, as did Katharine Wells in New York City. My wife Gail has read virtually everything in this volume at least once and has improved it considerably by her good sense and attention to detail. Jean Merritt typed the final draft with uncanny accuracy and superhuman patience, while Laura Proctor saved me from disaster repeatedly as I prepared the last revisions by computer. I am grateful to the two anonymous readers of the manuscript, who vetted it before publication and made a number of useful and well-founded suggestions for its improvement, and to Dr. Jane Fredeman, of the University of British Columbia Press, who gave the manuscript a thorough and welcome scrubbing, from which it emerged much improved and tidied. For help with the proofs I am indebted to my wife Gail and my student Michael Martin.

Institutions too are owed debts of gratitude. Scholarship support from the University of British Columbia, the Woodrow Wilson Foundation, and the Canada Council helped to keep me fed, housed, and supplied with books during the period when much of the foundation work was being done, and, more recently, the University of Victoria has forwarded my work by a series of faculty research grants, which have allowed me to gather materials too rare or too recent to have been available to me earlier. Finally, a grant from the Canadian Federation of the Humanities has aided publication of the volume itself. It should go without saying that many of the virtues of the book are due to the contributions of other people, including those just named, and that many of its defects might have been avoided had all of their advice been taken.

The book is dedicated to the memory of two people who, more than any others, helped and encouraged its author during much of the long period of its gestation. At the time of my very first attempts at translation—when I was still hesitating between Chinese poetry and French—it was Sharon Klein who saw to it that I had the use of a desk and typewriter, read and criticized my drafts, and extended the hospitality of her family to me when I had none of my own. Henry Wells and I never met personally, and our styles of translation and scholarship were as unlike as could be imagined, but our long correspondence was a continual source of pleasure and enlightenment. His warm encouragement, coming from a person of his broad interests and wide experience in literature, was of the greatest value to me for many years. It is a source of great regret that neither of these friends should have lived to see the all too modest product to which they contributed so much.

Earlier versions of some of the translations in this volume appeared in *Alcool*, the *Critical Quarterly*, *Ingluvin*, the *McGill Reporter*, and the *Malahat Review*, as well as in the anthology *Sunflower Splendor*, edited by Wu-chi Liu and Irving Lo (Anchor Books, 1975), to whom grateful acknowledgement is made.

University of Victoria
December, 1981

INTRODUCTION

The poems translated in this volume come from two collections of poetry written during the tenth century in a small and short-lived Chinese kingdom known in history as Southern T'ang, one of a number of minor states that flourished in southern China during the Five Dynasties, the brief and turbulent period (907–60) that spans the gap between the great ages of the T'ang (618–907) and Sung (960–1279). The first of these collections, the *Yang-ch'un Chi* ("Springtime"), consists of over a hundred lyrics by a courtier and official named Feng Yen-ssu (903–60), about half of which are translated here.[1] The second is the *Nan-T'ang Erh-chu Tz'u* ("Lyric Poems of the Two Lords of Southern T'ang"), which is translated in its entirety. Most of the thirty-odd poems in it are the work of Li Yü (937–78; r.961–75), the third and last ruler of the state, but the first four are by his father Li Ching (916–61; r.943–61), the second ruler. All of the poems are in a form called the *tz'u*, or "lyric," which was still in its earlier stages of development at the time.

Although their importance as poets is generally recognized, neither Feng Yen-ssu, who is usually thought a somewhat unsavoury character, nor Li Ching—because of the exiguity of his *oeuvre*—is an especially popular figure in Chinese literary history. Li Yü, in striking contrast, is one of the best known and most beloved of all Chinese poets. His popularity, which resembles that of Byron or Chopin in the West, is partly the result of the directness and apparent sincerity of the emotions that he expresses in his works, as well as of the relative lack of difficult passages caused by literary or historical allusions of the kind so common in most Chinese verse. But even more than this, his appeal to many readers is bound up with the storybook atmosphere that seems to pervade his life. He appears successively as a dashing and pampered young princeling, an accomplished artist and poet, a loving husband and father, a grief-stricken widower, a king oppressed by mighty foreign enemies whose destruction of his feeble state is inevitable, a desperately extravagant profligate, a prisoner-of-war in fear for his life, a forlorn and homesick captive, a helpless victim of court intrigue and pathological jealousy, and finally as a poet transcending personal anguish by embodying it in a few immortal lyrics, in which it is elevated to an expression of universal human experience. This emphasis on Li Yü's biography has had at least two undesirable consequences. For one thing, it has resulted in readers and scholars alike paying much more attention to Li than to Feng Yen-ssu, although close reading of Feng's poetry has convinced me that he is much closer to being Li's equal than the attention accorded him hitherto would suggest. A second consequence of the interest taken in Li Yü's biography is that it has tended to divert attention away from his own poems, except as they reflect on the biography. This is unfortunate too, because it encourages the notion that the merits of the poems are somehow dependent on the life of the poet and because it obscures, where it does not directly challenge, the fact that the poems themselves are—and this is a controversial point to which I shall return—almost entirely devoid of reliable autobiographical reference. For these reasons, and because historical research of recent decades has shown much of the traditional account of all three men's lives to be based on sources so late or so tendentious as to be of little use as biographical evidence, I have chosen to deal with their biographies as briefly as possible. All the same, a brief account of their lives and of the times in which they lived will help explain how they came to write the sort of poetry they did. Such an account will also provide an opportunity to correct a few of the more serious misunderstandings that have made their way into the traditionally accepted biographies.

The state of Southern T'ang was not, of course, the same as the T'ang dynasty proper, one of the great epochs of Chinese power and cultural greatness. Nor was it directly related to the T'ang by any generally accepted line of genealogical or administrative descent. It did, however, represent a conscious attempt to revive the tradition of T'ang authority, a rapidly fading memory by the time Li Ching's father established the state in 939. One attempt to restore it, the Later T'ang, founded by a Turk upon whom the T'ang surname (Li) had been conferred, had collapsed only a few years before, after controlling parts of northern China for little more than a decade. In reality, the strength of the T'ang court had begun to decline in 755, when the Rebellion of An Lu-shan (755–63) put an end to the T'ang's "golden age," the reign of Emperor Ming Huang (r.712–55). Although more than a century passed before the eruption of a rebellion of equal ferocity, the intervening period saw a steady weakening of the effectiveness of the central government as outlying areas came to be controlled to an increasing extent by provincial military governors whose loyalty to the throne was often only nominal. The most important area to remain under government control was the Yangtse basin, whose agricultural richness sustained the court long after many areas closer to the capital had ceased to contribute more than token amounts to the imperial treasury. As a consequence, the entrepôt city of Yang-chou, located near the junction of the Imperial Canal and the Yangtse, grew enormously in wealth and importance during this period. The later rebellion, led by a man named Huang Ch'ao, swept over most of China, including the Yangtse basin, during the years 875–85 and put an end to all but the faintest pretence of T'ang court rule. In fact, the year 907, which marks the legal end of the T'ang dynasty and its formal replacement by the first of the Five Dynasties (which controlled only the north of China), is significant not so much as the end of the T'ang, but rather as a sign that the restoration of centralized government had reached a stage that made the imperial throne once more an object of desire and a source of legitimacy, rather than a tarnished symbol of past glory in the midst of present anarchy.[2]

The process of reunification, however, was not complete until 978, when the last of the southern kingdoms was extinguished. In the interval, the constant warfare attendant on the re-establishment of court authority prevented all but the barest sort of cultural life from appearing in the north. In contrast, southern China enjoyed a remarkable degree of stability and peace through much of this period and, as a consequence, became at least temporarily the centre of Chinese literary and artistic life. Although there was a good deal of fighting in the south during the decade following the Huang Ch'ao Rebellion, by 895 the entire region (including Szechwan) had been divided into a limited number of clearly defined domains that were effectively independent, even though they generally recognized the formal status of the last puppet emperors of the T'ang until 907. Indeed, some continued to do so even later, for a declared allegiance to a non-existent court in the north was one of the more diplomatic ways of maintaining independence of its successors.

One of the largest and most prosperous of the southern states was that known as Wu, which occupied most of what is now the provinces of Kiangsu, Anhwei, and Kiangsi. The founder of Wu, Yang Hsing-mi, first appears in history as a local military leader active in the defence of his native district against Huang Ch'ao, but by 892 he had seized control of Yang-chou itself and emerged as the undisputed ruler of the entire lower Yangtse valley and as an independent prince in fact, if not yet in name. Although the sons of Yang Hsing-mi inherited the throne of Wu one by one after his death in 905, effective political control passed into the hands of one of Yang's trusted lieutenants, a man named Hsü Wen. Hsü Wen, in turn, trained a successor in the person of his adopted son Hsü Chih-kao, a foundling of unknown parentage who had been captured while still a child during one of Yang Hsing-mi's campaigns. Hsü Chih-kao succeeded to unchallenged control of Wu after the death of Hsü Wen in 927, but he did not actually usurp the throne until 937, after the death of the last of Hsü's sons. At first he called his new state Ch'i—an old name for Shantung, where he had been captured—but in 939 he renamed the state T'ang ("Southern" was added later by historians, in the interest of clarity) and changed his own name to Li Pien, declaring that he was actually an unrecognized descendant of one of the T'ang emperors.[3] This bold move implied an ambition to reunify all of China under his own control, and it may well have been "Li Pien's" intention to accomplish this, but the same cautious and methodical approach that had led him to delay his usurpation of the local throne for ten years presumably governed his strategy with regard to reuniting the Empire. Very probably he relied on living long enough to reap the harvest of his careful preparations, but he died in 943, after only a few years on the throne, leaving his newly founded kingdom—with some misgivings, it would appear—to his eldest son, Li Ching.

Li Ching had never been his father's favourite child, and perhaps conscious of this, he had repeatedly declined to accept the position of Heir Apparent. The events surrounding his succession are shrouded in uncertainty. One account alleges that "Li Pien" sent from his death-bed for a younger son, Ching-ta, intending to pass the throne on to him, only to have his messenger overtaken on the outskirts of the capital city by agents of Li Ching, who had been alerted to this change of heart by his father's doctor.[4]

Whatever the truth may be, Li Ching, often referred to later as *chung-chu*, or "middle ruler," was duly enthroned as King of T'ang in 943. His reign was not especially short, certainly not in comparison to those of many of his northern contemporaries, but neither was it particularly successful or happy. Conflicts between various court factions and among members of his own family were the source of much personal bitterness within his administration and finally led to bloodshed during the debacles of his last years. More serious in the long run was the deterioration of Southern T'ang's relations with the states that adjoined it. This is not the place to rehearse the sad tale of its invasions of Min (Fukien) and Ch'u (Hunan), the exploratory raids against the north, or the disastrous routs in which each of these ill-considered adventures ended; the results will suffice. To begin with, the wars of Li Ching's first decade on the throne wiped out much of the wealth that the state had accumulated during the prudent administrations of Yang Hsing-mi, Hsü Wen, and Hsü Chih-kao, leaving it poorly equipped to face the new challenges soon to arise. In addition, they demonstrated to all its neighbours that Southern T'ang was not only weak, but also troublesome. This was not critical so long as it was only one of a number of southern states of more or less comparable strength, but by the time Li Ching was ready to renounce his military escapades, the entire north had been brought back under the firm control of a centralized administration, whose next goal was naturally to recover the south. Threats and diplomatic pressures were followed in 956 by a massive invasion, during which much of the area north of the Yangtse, the Huai-nan region that had been Yang Hsing-mi's base, was overrun. The peace concluded in 958 represented a catastrophic defeat for Southern T'ang. The entire northern bank of the Yangtse, including the city of Yang-chou, was surrendered, and Li Ching was forced to accept tributary status, which required the presentation of a large yearly tribute payment to the northern court and the discontinuation of various practices, chiefly of ritual importance, that were proper only to independent states.

Li Ching and his state were spared a further onslaught, which was no doubt being planned in the north, by a last brief period of political uncertainty there that led to the founding of the Sung, successor to the last of the Five Dynasties. The first Emperor of Sung was a man of considerable experience and caution, who preferred to deal with his internal rivals before turning his attention to those outside. He consequently began by devoting his energies to a consolidation of his control of the civil and military apparatus in the north, postponing the reconquest of the south until the last years of his reign.

The respite from external pressures that this allowed was of little benefit to Li Ching, for the conclusion of peace abroad was followed by the outbreak of turmoil in court. The dominant faction, led by one Sung Ch'i-ch'iu (887–959) was purged in 958, and Sung himself was compelled to take his own life in the following year. Shortly afterward, the Heir Apparent, Hung-chi, Li Ching's eldest son, poisoned his uncle Ching-sui. Ching-sui had been Heir Presumptive earlier in Li Ching's reign and had continued to see to much of the business of government even later. Hung-chi met his own end within a month—perhaps unnaturally, remarks one astute historian. Ching-ta, the younger brother originally favoured by "Li Pien," had been defeated on the battlefield during the invasions from the north and sent out in disgrace to a provincial sinecure, where he seems to have devoted himself to the cultivation of an alcoholic stupor. And so Li Ching turned to a younger son, Li Yü, and made him the new Heir. Leaving Yü in charge in the capital, he moved his court to a remote town in the interior, Yü-chang (modern Nan-ch'ang, in Kiangsi). He was apparently hoping to begin the rebuilding of his state in this more secure territory—the northern armies were stationed within sight of the old capital—but his health failed instead, and he died not long after arriving in Yü-chang.

It is difficult now to form a clear impression of Li Ching's personality. The belligerent attitude of his regime may have reflected his own ambitions and poor judgment, or it may simply have been a policy of his advisers in which he acquiesced. The surviving anecdotes in which he figures personally tend to show his more important courtiers on somewhat familiar terms with him, perhaps because they were older men who had served his father for years before Ching, against the better judgment of some of them, had come to the throne. So little of his literary work survives that it is difficult to add much to our picture of him from it. The second of his two extant *shih* poems (see Appendix A) shows in its final image a turn of mind that is bizarre to say the very least. His four lyrics are of the highest quality, but not really distinctive, closely resembling those of Feng Yen-ssu in style.

If Li Ching does not emerge very clearly as a human being from the historical sources, the same cannot be said of Feng. And the personality that has been discovered in his case is not an attractive one. He is depicted in various anecdotes as a snob, a sycophant, a vengeful and unforgiving enemy, and the man responsible in considerable part for convincing Li Ching to adopt the aggressive foreign policy that eventually ruined his state. But it is very possible that he was not really as black as he has been painted. Hsia Ch'eng-t'ao and Lin Wen-pao, the two scholars who have studied Feng's life most extensively and carefully in recent times, are inclined to discount much of his traditional image. They point out that the surviving contemporary, or nearly contemporary, historical sources that are harshest in their criticism of Feng were heavily influenced by the opinions or writings of Feng's political opponents.[5]

Feng Yen-ssu is generally counted among the younger members of the faction led by Sung Ch'i-ch'iu, who had entered the service of Hsü Chih-kao as a young man. Chih-kao was anxious to build up a group of officials loyal to himself in anticipation of future conflicts at court, particularly with the sons of Hsü Wen. Sung Ch'i-ch'iu is mentioned as an adherent of Chih-kao as early as 917, and he was rarely far from power from that time until shortly before his death. Unfortunately for Feng Yen-ssu's later reputation, the earliest historical account of the Southern T'ang to survive, the *Tiao-chi Li-t'an* ("Idle Chats While Standing on the Fishing Pier") was written by the son of a man named Shih Hsü-pai, who felt that he had been wronged and his career ruined by Sung Ch'i-ch'iu.[6] The details of the conflict between Sung and Shih are uncertain, but it does appear to have been an example of friction between southerners established at court (in this case, Sung) and newly arrived refugees from the north who had hoped to start at the top. A similar conflict later arose between Feng Yen-ssu and a northerner named Sun Sheng.

Nursing his bitterness in unwelcome retirement, Shih Hsü-pai evidently formulated and passed on to his son an interpretation of Southern T'ang court politics that reflected his own misfortunes and the real or imagined injustices that he believed to have been inflicted on him. As often happens in such cases, he seems to have credited his "enemies" with greater malevolence and unity of purpose than were actually theirs. Shih's interpretation was not seriously challenged by Sung historians, for evidence of Southern T'ang's unworthiness to govern could only increase the justification for their own dynasty's extinction of it. But Lin Wen-pao's recent and detailed study of the various "factions" has demonstrated that they were neither so well organized nor so influential as Shih Hsü-pai would have had others believe. Hsü Chih-kao had, after all, usurped the throne after spending most of his life as a courtier himself. Both he and Li Ching were very careful to keep even their highest-ranking civil officials subordinate to a military commander chosen from the Royal Family.[7]

Once allowance has been made for the bias of some of the sources against Feng Yen-ssu, he emerges as a man of considerable wit and sophistication, though perhaps he displayed at times more of both than was either wise or diplomatic. He is said to have remarked of his rival Sun Sheng, "it's a shame to see golden platters and jade flagons brimming (*sheng*) with dog piss!" not only punning on Sun's personal name, which it was rude to use in speaking of him in the first place, but also perhaps alluding to his notorious practice of serving himself at dinner from dishes held by a bevy of singing girls, in lieu of a table (in one source it is Sun who makes the remark in referring to Feng, but this would miss much of the point).[8] In the *Tiao-chi Li-t'an* at least (and in sources derived from it), Sun Sheng has his revenge in a later confrontation. When Feng asks him, "What do you understand, that you should have been made a Minister?" Sun replies:

> I am only a poor scholar from east of the mountains. In bold writing and elegant composition I could not match you in ten lifetimes; in making jokes and drinking wine, not in a hundred; and I could not match you in fawning flattery or wicked tale-bearing if I were to live forever. All the same, when His Majesty assigned you to the establishment of the young prince [Feng had been Tutor to the Heir], it was his intention that you supervise and improve him with proper principles, not that you become his companion in whoring and gaming. Perhaps I do not understand anything; but what you understand may very well be the ruin of our state![9]

I have quoted this speech from a later source (Lu Yu's *History of Southern T'ang*), in which the *Tiao-chi Li-t'an* account is considerably amplified and embroidered upon. And, in fact, many of the more damning anecdotes concerning Feng Yen-ssu have taken shape in the same way, as Lin Wen-pao has shown. Moreover, such distortions of Feng Yen-ssu's reputation have tended to influence interpretations of his lyrics as well, for it is sometimes suggested that their subtlety and indirection reflect a courtier's uncertain, or indifferent, moral convictions.[10] In this sense, Li Yü has been by far the more controversial poet. The overwhelming impression of "sincerity" that his *tz'u* convey has made Chinese critics feel an urgent need, especially in modern times, to decide whether or not he was sincerely good. In Feng's case, they have been content to judge that he was probably devious and self-camouflaging by nature, just as his poetry is, and thus the question of his true character has been easier to deal with in a summary fashion. The most generous assessment is perhaps also the fairest. Committed to court service as a career, he found himself obliged to deal with men whose intelligence and sensitivity were far from equalling his own. Above all, it can be argued, he must have realized the hopelessness of Southern T'ang's prospects for survival. Especially after the repeated defeats in which Li Ching's various military adventures ended, he must have concluded with some bitterness that his only avenue for the achievement of enduring self-realization lay in the cultivation of the kind of literature of escape that the lyric represented.

Thus the details of his career are of only minor interest in themselves. His father had been in the service of Hsü Chih-kao, and Yen-ssu was in that of Li Ching by 937. Li made him an Academician upon his own succession to the throne in 943. Feng was made a Chief Minister in 946, in the midst of the campaigns against Min. In the following year he took responsibility for a crushing defeat that the forces of Southern T'ang had suffered and asked to be relieved of his post. This request was granted, and in 948 he was sent out to a provincial posting, where he remained until 951, when he resigned to observe mourning for his stepmother. By the spring of the next year, he was Chief Minister once again, only to step down briefly the next winter following the rout from Ch'u.[11] Restored to the Chief Ministership a few months later, he retained this office until the political upheavals of 958. Although several officials who had recently been prominent were put to death during the years 958–60, there is no suggestion in the historical sources that Feng's death was unnatural.

One of the charges made against Feng Yen-ssu, even in his own time, was that he owed his position in the government more to his literary talent than to any interest or ability in actual administration. Whatever the justice of this accusation, it is clearly consistent with what is known of the cultural atmosphere of the Southern T'ang court; weak as the state had proven to be militarily—and the worst was yet to come—it was without any doubt one of the most important cultural centres in China at the time, rivalled only by the successive kingdoms of Shu, in Szechwan. Literature and painting were the glories of the court. The poet Li Chien-hsün was one of the older statesmen remaining from the days of Hsü Chih-kao, while the younger generation included the brothers Hsü Hsüan (917–92) and Hsü Kai (921–74). Kai died just before the fall of Southern T'ang, but Hsüan survived to enjoy a modest career as an official and academic under the Sung dynasty. He is best known today for the standard edition of the old etymological dictionary *Shuo-wen Chieh-tzu* that he prepared, building on work done originally by his younger brother Kai, but he was also a poet of note, with a style reminiscent of Po Chü-yi. Another important early Sung philologist, Ch'en P'eng-nien (961–1017), who edited the standard rhyming dictionary *Kuang-yün*, grew up in Southern T'ang. He was at court while still a child, as a playmate for Li Yü's son, and later compiled a short historical work dealing with events and personalities of the state. In the field of painting, the genres of landscape, portraiture, and natural subjects were all cultivated, and Southern T'ang developments in each are generally thought to have laid the foundation for styles important, and in some cases dominant, during the Sung. The landscape painters Tung Yuan, active in the time of Li Ching, and Chü-jan, a monk from Southern T'ang who travelled to the Sung capital and became well known there after the fall of his native kingdom, are generally considered to be among the founders of the "Southern School" of landscape painting, which in time came to be regarded as the most distinguished tradition of all in that genre. Though in fact it seems that the two men may not have been so closely associated as later connoisseurs believed, both were important painters active in Southern T'ang. "Flower and bird" painting too was highly developed, Hsü Hsi being the leading master and an innovator whose style had far-reaching effects on later work in the genre. The Southern T'ang figure painter Chou Wen-chü, though a much more conservative artist stylistically, is still represented in modern collections by a few possibly genuine works. The artistic and literary achievements of Southern T'ang were complemented by highly developed ancillary crafts of several kinds, including paper and ink making and the carving of inkstones.[12]

Given this highly developed cultural milieu, it is not surprising that Li Yü (also called *hou-chu*, or "last ruler") took an active part in the creative life of the court. Even after some contemporary references are discounted as the flattery of his subordinates, it is clear that he was a man of very considerable talents in a variety of arts. The evidence of his poetry is, of course, still present in his surviving works. None of his paintings survive, and only one damaged and badly restored fragment of his calligraphy, but Sung dynasty connoisseurs praised his accomplishments in both arts, especially calligraphy. "The large characters are like split bamboo, the small ones like clusters of needles; altogether unlike anything done with a brush!" exclaimed one writer.[13] He was joined in his artistic and literary pursuits by his wife, the Empress Chou Chao-hui. She was particularly gifted in music, and a number of anecdotes recount incidents in which she demonstrated her talent for spontaneous composition.[14]

Li Yü and Chao-hui were married in 954, on the eve of the invasions from the north, when he was seventeen and she was eighteen. The marriage, which lasted until her early death in 964, seems to have been a happy and harmonious one. Indeed, it may well have been one of the few satisfying elements of Li Yü's middle years. Following the death of his father in 961, Li had succeeded to a throne for which he was neither suited by temperament nor prepared by training. He had grown up during days of relative security, if not of peace, with two older brothers and three capable uncles standing between him and succession to the throne. It is unlikely that anyone had ever expected him to rule the state, and so he did not have the kind of experience in administration that Li Ching had acquired as a youth. Neither had he held any military post during the wars. At least one courtier criticized his selection as Heir on the ground that he was a weakling inclined to place exaggerated confidence in Buddhist monks. But Li Ching, determined to preserve a regular succession, and perhaps mindful of the difficulties attendant on his own, refused the suggestion that one of Yü's younger brothers be named Heir instead.

In any case, it was no longer especially desirable to be King of T'ang. One of Li Yü's first acts as sovereign was to inform the Sung court—in language of extravagant humility—of his succession. In fact, the overriding concern of his entire reign was the necessity of handling relations with the Sung in such a way as to postpone the latter's insistence on complete capitulation. It was a task that the most resourceful of statesmen could not have succeeded in performing indefinitely, and it is perhaps more to Li Yü's credit than is generally recognized that he managed to put off the inevitable for fourteen years. His strategy, if that is the word, was simply to yield to all demands except one— that he himself move north and join the Sung court. The cost was heavy. Regular and irregular tribute payments drained the government treasury and burdened the hard-pressed peasantry. High officials had to accompany the tribute missions, and sometimes they were not allowed to return. One of Li Yü's younger brothers—the one recommended as Heir in his place—was also kept as a hostage in the Sung capital.

And other afflictions were in store. Chao-hui had borne Li two sons. The elder lived to serve the Sung dynasty in a minor official capacity, but the younger one died in 964 at the age of three.

When the Empress heard of it, she cried out in grief and collapsed, and from this time on declined without respite. Li Yü saw to her food himself morning and night, and she received no medicine that he had not tasted first. For many nights, he did not even so much as loosen the belt of his clothing to rest. Although the Empress's illness was very grave, she was still as alert as ever. She said to Li, "I have been very fortunate; since casting myself at your gate, I have been greatly favoured, and this has continued now for ten years. The honour of no woman can surpass this. All that is lacking is that our son has died in infancy and that now I too am dying and have no way to repay your goodness." Then she took the lute that Li Ching had presented to her and the jade bracelet that she always wore and personally handed them to Yü. In addition, she wrote out her will, asking to be buried simply. After three more days, she washed her face and straightened her clothing and makeup, placed a piece of jade in her mouth, and expired in the western chamber of the Jewel Radiance Palace.... Li mourned for her bitterly, until his bones stuck out and he could stand up only with the aid of a staff.[15]

Certainly the long dirge that Li Yü composed after Chao-hui's death would seem to confirm the sincerity of his grief (see Appendix A), but there is a conflicting account, or at the very least a complicating one. Li Yü was eventually remarried to Chao-hui's younger sister, known as Hsiao-Chou ("Younger Chou"). In one anecdote it is suggested that Li had brought her secretly into the Palace while Chao-hui was still ill. One day, Chao-hui caught sight of her sister, who was perhaps fourteen at the time, through a curtain:

> Shocked, she asked, "How long have you been here?" Hsiao-Chou was still very young and understood neither jealousy nor suspicion, and so she replied, "Several days already!" The Empress was enraged, and did not, to the moment of her death, again turn her face away from the wall. Yü was very distressed, and tried to cover up the incident.[16]

Now, it is difficult, not to say impossible, to reconcile Chao-hui's gracious death-bed farewell speech to Li Yü, as recorded in the first of these anecdotes, with her furious withdrawal in the second. Much of her speech—in fact, much of the entire first account of her illness and death—is heavily indebted to the conventions of edifying feminine biography in the Chinese style. The second anecdote is somewhat more plausible, and in any case there seems to be little doubt that Hsiao-Chou was in the palace long before she formally became Yü's second wife in 968. Yet it appears—more from the *shih* poems written after Chao-hui's death than from the hysterical, but entirely conventional, grief of the dirge—that Li Yü was genuinely afflicted by her passing. Of course, it is quite possible, given the tendentious character of so much of the historiography of the period, that either or both of the anecdotes is fictitious in part or as a whole. But the ability to pursue simultaneously two conflicting goals while feeling perfectly sincere in one's devotion to both is perhaps more common than is often realized. Whatever the inherent likelihood of either account taken by itself, there is no real necessity to choose between them.

Li Yü's mother died less than a year after Chao-hui, and the requirements of the official mourning period delayed his formal marriage to Hsiao-Chou until 968. The ceremony, when it did take place, is said to have been the occasion of some barbed comments from the assembled courtiers, but Li Yü took them in good part. Indeed, one has the impression that by this time he had given up all pretence of preserving his royal dignity. His extravagances multiplied apace. Some were intended to amuse his new wife; others, to demonstrate his increasing favour of the Buddhist clergy.[17] Although the lavishness of his expenditures is a staple theme of early Sung discussions of his reign, these ought to be treated with some caution. In many cases, his character and fate were being used as an object lesson in support of early Sung austerity policies, as well as justification of the Sung conquest of his state. The stern note that the Sung historians sound in discussing Li's amusements has an ironic ring to later readers, who know that the Northern Sung itself collapsed before an invasion by nomads from the north in the days of Emperor Hui-tsung, a man whose artistic preoccupations and style of life resembled those of Li Yü in many ways.

An example of the way Li Yü's image in history has been tarnished is the theory that he was responsible for the introduction of footbinding in China. Most works on the subject, whether in Chinese or in Western languages, assume this to be the case.[18] It has even found a place in imaginative literature (in one Chinese collection of supernatural tales, Li's ghost laments its sufferings in Hell as a result of his introduction of this cruel practice).[19] But a critical examination of early sources rather mitigates his guilt, if it does not entirely exonerate him. All that the earliest source says is that among his palace consorts was one who performed a dance on a raised stage shaped like a golden lotus blossom, her feet being bound with ribbons into the shape of a crescent moon. There is no reference whatever to the permanent deformation of women's feet from childhood, and, in fact, the dance, as it is described, would have been difficult or impossible to perform with feet bound in the later fashion. What the anecdote may refer to is something more like Western "toe" shoes. The imprecision of the original account aside, it seems unlikely for two reasons that this particular custom can be blamed on Li Yü. In the first place, the earliest source for the story is an anonymous collection of anecdotes from the late Northern Sung (c.1120) whose unreliability has been demonstrated in other cases.[20] In the second, and more important, Li Yü's reputation would surely have precluded the adoption on any wide scale of so egregiously wasteful and inhumane a custom as footbinding, done simply in imitation of him. If anything, the opposite would likely have been the case. It should be obvious that footbinding owes its origin to social and economic conditions of much broader importance and force than the supposed perversions of a man widely dismissed in Sung times as a discredited libertine.

A more serious problem for Li Yü than the shape of his consorts' feet was the condition of his state. A disappointed office-seeker fled north to the Sung in 970 taking with him charts of Yangtse River crossing points that he had surveyed while living in retirement in the guise of a monk or a fisherman. The Sung court rewarded the man with high office, and his charts may indeed have been used for the eventual construction of the floating bridge across the Yangtse over which the Sung armies·passed only a few years later. This incident suggests that the future of Southern T'ang was widely regarded as being very short. Several of Li Yü's officials presented plans for a counter-offensive or at least for a reform of government policies in order to strengthen the state, but all who did so were rebuffed, and several even lost their lives, for Li no longer dared show any public interest in resistance to Sung authority.

Finally, in 974, an envoy arrived with a direct request for Li Yü to present himself at court in the Sung capital. When he declined to do so, on grounds of ill health, the long prepared invasion was launched. By the following spring,

virtually all of the cities along the Yangtse had been taken by the Sung armies
and the capital itself was surrounded and besieged. The city surrendered in
975, and Li Yü and a party of his family members and high officials were
transported up the Grand Canal to the Sung capital in mid-winter, arriving
early in 976. Dressed in white clothing and a gauze cap, symbolic of
preparation for death, he was taken to the Pavilion of Radiant Virtue to await
the Sung emperor's disposition of his case. This proved to be much less severe
than might have been expected. He was not executed, but given a residence in
the capital and kept there under house arrest. In the course of the year he
received the uncomplimentary title "the Recalcitrant Marquis." Several of his
officials, including Hsü Hsüan, accepted posts in the Sung bureaucracy.

Thus Li Yü began the two and a half years of captivity during which he is
often thought to have written most of his best poems. While his life had been
spared, he was reduced to circumstances that he could hardly have imagined
during the years before his capture. Some of his palace women were taken
into the Imperial harem; others drifted away to become entertainers. An often
quoted note to one of them still in the south read, "In this place I do nothing
day and night but wash my face in tears."[21] After a year or so of confinement,
he complained of poverty and was granted additional funds. He was
summoned several times to converse with the emperor or to attend social
functions at court. Those that have been recorded were occasions of
humiliation or insult. The Sung emperor once turned to an aide, after Li had
recited a poem of his own composition in response to a command, and said
pointedly, "What a perfect Academician!" While showing Li around his
library, the emperor said, "Many of these books used to belong to you. Have
you been doing much reading lately?" Hsiao-Chou too was taken into the
inner palace several times, and the hysterical scenes that took place after each
return caused Li a great deal of discomfort.[22]

It is often said that Li Yü was poisoned on the order of the second Sung
emperor, and a number of anecdotes purport to supply background to this
incident, but a recent study by Juan T'ing-cho has shown that these are later
fabrications. Actually, both the first and second emperors showed quite
remarkable lenience in their treatment of the various surrendered southern
kings. The latter and their relatives were supported at public expense or
appointed to government posts, and their former officials—Hsü Hsüan is a
typical example—were employed according to their abilities. Li Yü seems to
have lived in reasonable comfort, though not, of course, with anything like the
establishment he had maintained while a king. The most reliable sources
report that his death was due to a chronic illness rather than poison.[23]

Now, the relevance of Li Yü's life to the study of his poetry has rarely been
questioned. So far as the *shih* poems and the prose works are concerned, this
seems a reasonable assumption, for most of the few extant works in these

forms owe their very survival to their citation in early historical sources as explicitly biographical material. But with the *tz'u* the ground is much less sure. Most *tz'u* poems prior to Li's time were written by men who adopted the literary persona of young courtesans or at least took such women as their subject matter. Some of Li's *tz'u* give the impression of being more personal in their reference, and this has led to the concoction of elaborate accounts of his inner life based on the assumption that all of the lyrics can be taken in this way. Such an account runs something like this:

> Li Yü's lyrics can be divided into three [sometimes it is two, or even four] groups on the basis of their content, and these groups correspond to the major divisions of his life. That is, there are, to begin with, the carefree and exuberant poems of his youth, before he came to the throne, in which he celebrates the luxurious and unrestrained life that he enjoyed as a pampered prince. Then, there are the sadder poems of his middle period, when he was beset by the cares of state and afflicted by the successive deaths of his son, wife, and mother. Finally, there are the great lyrics of his last years in captivity, in which he pours out his homesickness and remorse. Of course we know that he was happy in his youth, for example, because we have those carefree and exuberant poems that he must have written then because that was when he was so carefree and exuberant, as the poems show....

And so it goes. The ingenuous circularity of all this is little short of breath-taking, while its ubiquity in the secondary literature is enough to make one despair of literary scholarship. In point of fact, with one possible exception to be considered shortly, none of the lyrics can be dated precisely. Anecdotes preserved in early historical sources—that is, ones compiled within a half-century or so of Li's death—do associate certain lyrics with specific incidents. The "P'u-sa Man" poems (XX, XXII, XXIII), for example, are said to celebrate Yü's clandestine affair with Hsiao-Chou. Now, it does seem a little far-fetched to suppose that the ruler of a state the size of Southern T'ang would actually have—or be able—to lurk about unattended in his own garden in the small hours of the night in order.to contrive a secret tryst with a young woman who could not possibly have been spending the night anywhere in the inner palace except on the understanding that she was available to its royal occupant. That, after all, is the point of the story of Chao-hui's death-bed fury. Still less is it likely that, having gotten away with the tryst, he would have immediately "written it up." A few of these anecdotal attributions may have had some basis, but they hardly constitute proof, and still less do they justify the sort of general distribution of all the lyrics among a limited number of very crudely delimited biographical periods that is commonly advanced as demonstrated fact.[24]

What is possible, of course, and what may actually be referred to by this anecdote, is that Li Yü composed these lyrics on the highly conventional theme of secret lovers' meetings for the entertainment of Hsiao-Chou, perhaps during a song-writing game in the course of a banquet. But to admit this possibility is to cast serious doubt upon the entire exercise of interpreting the poems as autobiographical documents, for even the poems that seem most plausibly attributed to Li Yü's years in captivity then become suspect. The expression "old kingdom" (*ku-kuo*), for example, naturally taken as a reference to Li's former domain, and thus as evidence that the poems in which it occurs (V, VIII) were written during the period of his imprisonment in the north, is extensively used in the writing of all sorts of poets, none of whom were ever rulers of anything and in whose writings the expression simply means "native district" or "home town." A few of Li Yü's lyrics can be attributed with reasonable certainty either to the period of captivity or to the thirty-odd years before on purely textual grounds—that is, from what is recorded about the manuscript sources from which they were collected—but judged strictly on the grounds of content, most of the poems could possibly have been written at any time during his adult life. In saying this, I have in mind not so much the "old kingdom" poems, which I am quite prepared to admit are most plausibly assigned to his last years, but rather the supposedly "early" works, whose romantic exuberance, precisely because it is entirely conventional, could reflect their composition during the period of enforced idleness while under house arrest in the Sung capital just as well as it could a state of mind arbitrarily assigned to Li Yü's youth, about which, in fact, very little is known.

The single exception to the scepticism that I propose is of course poem XXXVI, which purports to describe Li's tearful farewell to his old palace. The authenticity of the poem has been challenged on the ground that it is found in a book—the *Tung-p'o Chih-lin* ("Su Tung-p'o's Grove of Tales")—often believed to be a forgery misattributed to the great Sung writer and statesman Su Shih. But this challenge rests on the assumption that if a book was not actually written by the person whose name is on the title page, then nothing in it can be true. This, of course, is no more the case than its opposite, that one can believe anything, provided that it is found in a document actually written by the person to whom it is attributed. In any case, as Kung Ying-tê pointed out quite correctly over forty years ago, the spurious character of the *Tung-p'o Chih-lin* is by no means proven.[25] To my mind, a more serious ground for doubt about the authenticity of the lyric is the distinctiveness of its vocabulary. Only one of the words most commonly used in the other lyrics of Li Yü occurs in this poem, and fully one-third of those that do occur are found in no other poem reliably attributed to him, a much higher fraction than can be derived from study of the vocabulary of any other poem translated in this volume.[26] One's attention is also drawn to the position of this poem in the

Nan-T'ang Erh-chu Tz'u, where it follows the group of poems known to the compiler(s) only from manuscript copies. This might imply that it was thought to be somehow less reliable an attribution than others, but the arrangement of the collection is a complex problem about which it would be premature to draw firm conclusions. So far as the question of vocabulary is concerned, if the poem were actually autobiographical in intent, then the uncharacteristic usage might be readily explained, and since this is the very question at issue, little more can be concluded with regard to it.

In sum, few, if any, of these poems can be directly related to actual events or moods in the life of Li Yü, and the same is true, naturally, of the lyrics of Li Ching and Feng Yen-ssu as well. Part of the reason for this lies in the nature of the *tz'u* itself, and thus it may be useful to look next at the origins of the form and to examine the highly developed world of moods and imagery that had become associated with it by the time of the Southern T'ang poets. The best way to throw the special characteristics of the *tz'u* into sharper relief is to compare an example with one in the traditional *shih* form (that used by such well-known poets as T'ao Ch'ien, Wang Wei, Li Po, and Po Chü-yi). The points to be made are sufficiently general that almost any examples of the two forms would be sufficient for the purpose.[27] The two examined here are by Li Yü, his *tz'u* lyric to "Yi Hu Chu" (VII) and his *shih* poem "Jotted Down on the Tenth Day of the Ninth Month" (XIII in Appendix A). The first difference between the two is evident before considering the poems proper. While the *shih* poem has a title, which purports, at least, to inform us directly of the occasion for writing it, the *tz'u* is headed simply by "To 'Yi Hu Chu.' " "Yi Hu Chu," which means "one pot of pearls," has no direct connection with the matter of the poem, in which neither pot nor pearls are to be found, but, rather, is the name of a melody to which the words were originally written. On the simplest level the difference in "title" means from the start that the *shih* poem will be, or at the very least will pretend to be, about the poet's experience or reflection on a specific occasion. "Yi Hu Chu," in contrast, is simply a direction to the performer. One will only find out what the poem is about after beginning to read or listen to it.

Two additional formal differences between *shih* and *tz'u* are more immediately evident in the Chinese original than in a translation. To begin with, while the lines of the *shih* poem are equal in length (seven characters per line), the lines of the *tz'u* are uneven, having four, five, or seven characters each. The particular sequence found in this poem (4+7+7+4+5 7+7+7+4+5) is derived from the original "Yi Hu Chu" melody; other melody patterns have entirely different formulae. Moreover, the *tz'u* poem is divided into two stanzas (presumably reflecting a repetition of the music), while the *shih* is not.[28]

The differences between *shih* and *tz'u*, however, go beyond these few, which are all related to the musical origins of the latter. There is also a difference in the basic elements from which the poems are constructed. A particular characteristic of *shih* poetry is that poems in this form are made up of couplets, rather than of lines or stanzas. There are several different types of *shih*, and the structural requirements for the couplets vary from one to another. Our example is the relatively demanding type known as "regulated verse." In this form, in addition to strict prosodic prescriptions that govern the tonal pattern of each line, it is required that the lines of the two internal couplets be semantically parallel. Thus, "yellow" matches "red," "blossoms" matches "leaves," and so forth, although it is not always possible to reflect this parallelism in English translation. The essential point is not the parallelism itself, for it is not required in other types of *shih* and occasionally occurs in *tz'u*; nor is it the prosodic requirements, which again are looser in other types of *shih* and have their analogues in the *tz'u*. Rather, it is that all the formal requirements of the *shih* are tied to the couplet, while in the *tz'u* it is the line and the stanza that are essential. Some of the implications of all these differences will be discussed later. But it should be noticed here how much more flexible the *tz'u*'s narrative flow is compared to the more formal, at times almost mosaic, quality of the *shih*. The *shih* also goes much more carefully about setting a scene, furnishing it with appropriate images and reflections, and finally drawing a specific conclusion. In the *tz'u*, it is clear that there is some lapse of time between the scenes described in the two stanzas, but aside from this there is an improvised quality to the description that is quite different from what is found in the *shih*. The differences between the *shih* and the *tz'u* naturally lead to questions about how the latter form originated and how it came, since it appears to have been a popular or folk form at first, to be taken up by princes and courtiers. Unfortunately, conclusive answers to these questions are impossible to obtain, and even thoroughly to survey what is known would go well beyond immediate concerns. Very little non-elite poetry has been preserved from the T'ang dynasty, the period during which the *tz'u* developed. While the individual poems that have been lost were presumably just as inane and inconsequential in themselves as the lyrics to modern popular songs, their disappearance is to be regretted all the same, for, lacking them, it is necessary to rely to a considerable extent upon hypothesis and inference in an attempt to reconstruct the early history of the *tz'u*.

It does seem likely that the purely formal elements of the *tz'u* had an origin separate from that of their thematic content and that the former are derived in large part from the music to which the early *tz'u* were set. From what is known of music during the T'ang dynasty, it seems likely that many of the melodies were of Central Asian origin, and it has been suggested that the irregularity of the lines in *tz'u* derives from the unequal phrase lengths of the non-Chinese tunes. This explanation is perhaps simplistic, for it ignores the likely case that words were repeated or held over for more than one note in performance (it may even contain an ethnocentric assumption that barbarian music must necessarily have been less regular than that of the Chinese). But the simple fact that Central Asian music was popular in T'ang times is sufficient to make it plausible that some *tz'u* melodies at least were derived from it.

Whatever the formal origin of the *tz'u*—and the details are still a matter of scholarly debate—their conventional themes clearly seem to have come from native traditions that predated the T'ang.[29] One of these was the "boudoir lament." Although apparently of popular origin, these poems had been cultivated by the educated class since the third century at least. They characteristically depicted the beauty and solitary longing of a lonely wife whose husband was away on military service or of a neglected palace lady. In some cases the woman in these poems was intended to stand for the poet, insufficiently appreciated or rewarded by his social or political superiors, but often the poems were simply literary exercises. This was especially true in the sixth and seventh centuries, when a courtly literary tradition that valued subtlety and artifice dominated the world of poetry. The descriptive and mildly erotic nature of the boudoir lament made it an ideal vehicle for court poetry, spurring poets on to ever greater heights (or depths) of indirection and impersonality. These poems, written in what came to be called the "palace style" (*kung-t'i*), never went entirely out of fashion, but the classic anthology devoted to them, the *New Chants of the Jade Terrace* (*Yü-t'ai Hsin-yung*), was compiled around 550 and tended to define the genre for later poets. Much of the luxurious imagery characteristic of earlier *tz'u* poetry is derived from these poems.[30]

A second tradition that contributed to the formation of the *tz'u* was a popular genre, the "Southern Songs," many of which are associated with the name of a legendary singing-girl named Tzu-yeh ("Midnight"). These songs were short, often witty or erotic, poems celebrating the courtesans of the warm southern regions of China during the Six Dynasties period (fourth to sixth centuries; a few of the poems translated here were even written to a melody called "Tzu-yeh Song"). It is probable that the Southern Songs did not disappear as a living popular tradition after the establishment of the T'ang, even if we have little direct evidence for them after that.[31] Certainly courtesans and singing-girls were an important part of the T'ang entertainment world. There is good reason to believe that they went on making up or adopting new songs throughout the dynasty, singing them to the newly current foreign music, but presumably retaining much of the traditional subject matter for their lyrics.[32] Among the T'ang manuscripts discovered in the grottos of Tun-huang early in this century, for example, was a fragmentary collection of anonymous popular *tz'u* poems probably written down in the ninth century.[33]

It is not clear just when the educated elite of China began to compose lyrics in the *tz'u* form. Although there are a few true *tz'u* attributed to such famous T'ang poets as Li Po (701–62) and Po Chü-yi (772–846), the authenticity of these poems is very dubious.[34] The first major poet to compose extensively in the *tz'u* form seems to have been Wen T'ing-yün (813?–70), whose luxurious, essentially impersonal lyrics are known for their success in capturing the fragile and temporary quality of the courtesan's life. Here, for example, is a lyric that he wrote to the melody "Keng-lou-tzu".

> Golden swallow hairpins,
> A rouged and powdered face:
> Among the blossoms we meet for only a moment.
> You know my thoughts;
> I am moved by your tenderness;
> Heaven alone may answer for this love.
>
> Incense in ripened stalks,
> Candlewax running in tears:
> As though to match the thoughts in our two hearts.
> My coral pillow is damp;
> My brocade coverlet cold,
> I awake as the water-clock runs down....[35]

The detailed and brightly illuminated setting of this monologue is its only apparent substance. It has no argument, but consists rather of a series of images and sentiments only vaguely attached to the hairpin-crowned face of its opening lines. At the time that poems such as this one were first being composed, it was no doubt the music to which they were sung that held the attention of their audiences, the lyrics being only a secondary element.

But Wen T'ing-yün was an important poet in the orthodox forms. That he should have taken up this new form and become the first poet to make a permanent contribution to its history as serious literature cannot have been the result of his celebrated loose-living alone. Nor can the sudden flowering of the *tz'u* in the next century, during which numerous poets took up the form and its conventions with such dedication that "T'ang *shih* and Sung *tz'u*" has become a cliché of literary history, have been the result merely of caprice. The explanation commonly given is that the *shih* was "used up" and that a new form was bound, in some vaguely organic or even Darwinian way, to replace it, as though it were some sort of poetic trilobite or pterodactyl.[36] But this is a vulgar error of the crudest sort, one that the enormous vitality of the *shih* tradition in the Sung and later periods should be more than sufficient to discredit. It might be better to view the rise of the *tz'u* as a literary development conditioned in part by broader changes that were taking place at this time in the nature of the Chinese literate elite and its relationship to political power.

The near monopoly over high-ranking administrative posts that members of old aristocratic clans had long enjoyed began to be weakened late in the seventh century, after Empress Wu modified the system of competitive civil service examinations in order to extend access to high rank to persons of relatively humble origin.[37] The extent to which this reform alone actually diminished the influence of the aristocrats as persons has probably been overestimated, but it now seems quite clear that the literati had come by the end of the eighth century to think of themselves in a new way; that is, even those who were of aristocratic birth felt the need to validate their high status by success in the official literary examinations. Thus they gradually came to identify themselves as scholar-officials rather than as aristocrats. It is this new seriousness of their identification of status with literary and intellectual accomplishments in an orthodox tradition that distinguishes such Middle T'ang writers as Han Yü, Po Chü-yi, and Yuan Chen and defines at the same time the tragedy of those who failed in their careers as statesmen, most notably Liu Tsung-yuan.

With the breakdown of central government control and the near disappearance of the scholar-officials' prospects to participate effectively in the administration of "all under heaven," however, they were forced to evolve a new self-image, one more consonant with their new roles. The central fact of professional life for the late T'ang literati was that the imperial court was no longer the only seat of political power or administration in China. Less territory under the control of the court meant, quite simply, fewer government jobs to be filled. One result was that men unable to secure an appointment in the central government bureaucracy were forced, in increasing numbers, to seek employment in the service of provincial governors or military men who were still loyal to the central government but who maintained their own staff organizations outside the framework of the established hierarchy of local administration.[38] Even in the mid-eighth century, the poet Ts'en Shen, who came from a very distinguished family, took service as an aide to a series of generals active in campaigns in what is now Chinese and Soviet Turkestan.[39]

The sort of person capable of exercizing the quasi-military authority required by the times was unlikely to have had either the opportunity or the inclination to acquire an elegant literary style. But the prestige of letters remained high, and so educated men were engaged by them as secretaries or administrative assistants. A writer so employed was often more than just a subordinate of his employer. If he was at all well known, he might be one of the ornaments of the latter's establishment, treated like an honoured guest.

And thus the demands on his literary talents might well extend beyond office hours. He could find himself called upon at banquets, during which courtesans naturally entertained, to supply elegant lyrics for the currently popular tunes. The most powerful of these locally prominent officials were those stationed in Yang-chou, in the heart of the land that had given rise to the original "Southern Songs," which may help to explain the re-emergence of many of the old themes and images at this time. Certainly the splendour of Yang-chou, and especially of its courtesans, became legendary during this period, and it seems reasonable to suppose that this confluence of local literary tradition, economic and cultural prosperity, and romantic opportunity played a large part in the poems written on such occasions. The occasional nature of the poems would not encourage their preservation, especially if they were in a "popular" form. It does seem clear, from preserved lists of musical titles of late T'ang date, that some of the melodies to which later *tz'u* poems were written were already part of the repertoire of entertainers in the capital. Thus it may have been in Ch'ang-an rather than in Yang-chou that the final combination of foreign music with old southern themes took place. Poignant nostalgia for the south is, in any event, a prominent theme in the early *tz'u*, antedating Li Yü's adoption of it as an autobiographical motif (if such it was), and Wen T'ing-yün's lyrics should probably be read as having emerged from such a milieu.

It was only when the T'ang central government broke down completely, and certain of the provincial governors' establishments found themselves *de jure*, as well as *de facto*, independent princely courts, that the *tz'u* lyrics composed by their retainers, now courtiers, began to be regarded as in some sense "respectable" writings. This happened first in the state of Shu, located in what is now Szechwan. One of the literati refugees from central China instrumental in founding this state was a man named Wei Chuang (836–910), who is generally regarded as the second major *tz'u* poet, after Wen T'ing-yün. His example seems to have set the fashion in the new kingdom, for it was in Shu, thirty years after Wei's death, that the earliest known anthology of literati *tz'u* was collected. This compilation, the *Hua-chien Chi* ("Among the Blossoms"), is still extant today, and the five hundred lyrics that it contains constitute the largest single body of surviving pre-Sung *tz'u* poetry.

Wen T'ing-yün and Wei Chuang occupy places of honour in the *Hua-chien Chi*, but most of the poems are by poets of a younger generation, all but a few of them officials in the service of Shu. In general, these men modelled their style on that of Wen T'ing-yün, rather than on the somewhat drier, more narrowly personal lyrics of Wei Chuang. The lyrics of the Southern T'ang poets to which this volume is devoted are generally quite different in style from those of the Shu poets.[40] Many of them, of course, were written after the compilation of the *Hua-chien Chi* in 940, for the Southern T'ang poets were all active somewhat later. But the difference is not necessarily caused simply by the passage of time. It may well be that their works grew out of a tradition, perhaps not one with a long history, distinct from that exemplified by Wen T'ing-yün, whose lyrics must, after all, have been somewhat old-fashioned by 940. The nature of this stylistic difference will be looked at later, but first the *tz'u* should be examined more closely as a poetic form.

Tz'u poetry has, in general, been less enthusiastically received in the West than has that in the *shih* form, in part as a result of a lack of understanding of the conventions that lie behind it. Take, for example, this lyric by Niu Hsi-chi, one of the *Hua-chien* poets:

To "Yeh Chin Men"

As autumn draws to an end;
One after another, high mountains and branching roads.
Where have they gone, the neighing horse and cracking whip?
Dawn birds and frost fill the trees....

A dream is broken by bells and drums in the Forbidden City;
Tears drop without number on a sandalwood pillow.
One dab of pink frozen anew in thin mist:
Raven brows with sorrow they cannot express.[41]

Now, it requires a more extensive background to understand the imagery and surface argument of this poem than one might at first suppose. If a reader does not know, for example, that a neighing horse or a branching road implies imminent farewell, and a cracking (literally "waving") whip the last sight of a departing friend or lover, that drums were sounded to mark off the hours of the night and bells at dawn, that sandalwood was a precious substance, that pillows were customarily made of wood or some other solid material, or that T'ang ladies powdered their faces, rouged their cheeks, and painted their eyebrows, then this lyric will miss much of its effect. This sort of information is essential to an understanding of the poetry, but it is likely to be more distracting than enlightening if presented in bits and pieces in the form of footnotes to the individual poems. To avoid this sort of distraction as much as possible—some poems do include specific references better explained as they occur—the world of the *tz'u* and its imagery should be considered as a whole at this point.

In fact, there are several distinct problems to be dealt with. One is the sort of background information just alluded to. Another is the larger, and eventually more significant, question of what these lyrics "mean" and how this meaning is conveyed. And the peculiar nature of modern Western ideas about artistic originality and individuality raises crucial questions that must be faced if these poems are to enjoy the appreciation that they deserve.

First the world of the *tz'u* must be considered.[42] Perhaps the first thing necessary to know is something of the Chinese year and its symbols. Whatever *tz'u* poets did in the summer—hot and humid in southern China—they did not write poems about it. Winter too appears only rarely, and then generally as a season foretold by the first cool of autumn or one recalled by the fading chill of spring. The two seasons for poetry are spring and autumn. Spring is associated with the east in Chinese cosmology, and the east wind brings with it "spring fever," as Westerners might call it. Autumn, of course, is the opposite of spring. Its direction is west and its meaning is old age and death. In fact, autumn was, in traditional China, the preferred season for war and executions. A day is thought of as a year in microcosm, and thus it is dawn and dusk that appear most often in the poetry. The daytime sun appears rarely—Li Yü's "Huan Hsi Sha" is an exception—but the moon is everywhere. Sometimes it is the full moon lighting up the world with its haunting white glow; elsewhere it is the new (or very old) moon—a thin crescent reminiscent of a beautiful woman's eyebrow, seen of course low in the west at dusk or in the east just at daybreak after a long night.

The seasons bring with them a recurrent round of experience: the late snow that sets off the purity of evergreen bamboo, the early plum blossoms that explode with delicate and short-lived colour before winter is completely over, the trailing willows of early spring, turning hazily yellow-green and putting forth their floating catkins. As spring turns warmer, lush fragrant annuals (*ts'ao*) reappear, and soon grow in thick sweet-smelling clumps visited by fluttering butterflies. While the weather is still cool and damp, songbirds— swallows, sparrows, orioles—appear and build their nests, working in pairs that remind the personae of these poems of their own lonely solitude. As spring draws to an end, driving rains crush the last faded blossoms into mud and often spoil the weather for Ch'ing-ming and Cold Food, the spring festivals.

As we have remarked, summer is passed over in silence. With the approach of autumn, rushes flower in white plumes along every waterway, and cicadas and crickets trill deafeningly in gardens and fields. Mist gathers overnight, and chrysanthemums and dogwood flower in time for Double Nine, the festival of late autumn, when people climb to a high place to drink an infusion of chrysanthemums steeped in wine in the hope of defying winter, as the flowers do, and enjoying a long life. As the beauty of autumn fades in turn, geese appear in the sky flying south for the winter. Since they are thought to carry messages from distant loved ones, their coming reminds people of those far away from whom no word has come (fish too were thought of as letter carriers). Also prominent in autumn is the *wu-t'ung*, or "phoenix tree," whose heart-shaped leaves provided a symbol for lovesickness and whose straight trunk was seen as so symbolic of strength of character that it was believed the legendary phoenix would roost in no other tree. In autumn too, rain-swollen rivers stream inexorably to the east—a geographical accident that takes on added emotional significance from its contrast with the equally inexorable westward motion of heavenly bodies and, in the larger sense of the direction west, the course of the year and of human life.

It is within such a round of seasonal symbols and images that the women depicted in the *tz'u* pass their lives. Much of the imagery of the poems, though, evokes their material surroundings. These are unfailingly luxurious, for the emotional desolation of the women derives part of its power from the opulence with which they are housed and clothed. The imagery is based in large part on conventions established centuries earlier by the poets of the *Jade Terrace* anthology. Although the illusion that she is an inmate of the palace is sometimes maintained, the girl in the poems is clearly a courtesan of the highest class. Her value thus lies in her physical allure above all, to the extent that whatever artistic or intellectual accomplishments she may acquire are of little avail once her beauty has faded except to while away the long and solitary hours. Typically she plays a lute (*ch'in*, actually a kind of zither), an instrument especially suited to solitary self-expression.

She lives, as does her Western counterpart, in a "house" (usually called *lou*, "pavilion"—a building of more than one storey) or a wineshop. These are sometimes referred to by elegantly allusive names, such as Shamanka Hill (*wu-shan*), where an early Chinese king was supposed to have spent a night with the goddess of "morning clouds and evening rain" (sexual intercourse), or Resplendent Terrace (*chang-t'ai*), the old Gay Quarter of Ch'ang-an, the T'ang capital. Sometimes a woman is said to live in Chao-yang Palace, the residence of Emperor Ch'eng of the Han dynasty's favourite consort Ho-te after she had displaced her elder sister Flying Swallow in the emperor's affections. Inside the latticed windows, often screened with coloured gauze and shaded by blinds that roll up and are held by jade hooks, she is seen in her elaborately furnished boudoir. The bed is spread with embroidered coverlets, which often prove too thin for comfort on cold nights spent alone. Around the bed are standing screens, usually adorned with a painting of some appropriate subject, such as mandarin ducks ("bridal ducks"), a symbol of fidelity in marriage. The room is naturally equipped with a mirror, in which the signs of approaching age are reflected as clearly as the charm of youth. The air is heavy with incense, often burnt in blocks made in the shape of animals. Incense was burned for its own sake and also used to scent clothing, which was hung on a large wicker-work frame over a censer. As pervasive as the aroma of incense is the dripping of a clepsydra, or water-clock, most noticeable during the still hours of late night or early morning as it relentlessly marks off the passage of time. A further reminder of time, during the night at least, is the drum beaten to mark off the watches. This is heard from somewhere in the distance.

But if the drum is a sign from the outside world, it is from a world that the woman herself is rarely seen to visit, except for the occasional party held on a "painted boat." Her contract with the life of ordinary women is limited to hearing the sound of their fulling mallets in autumn, as they prepare winter clothing for their absent husbands, away perhaps fighting on the distant frontiers. The woman of these poems spends hours simply leaning against the railing of her balcony, watching the sunset, the moon, the breeze in a nearby grove, or the passage of the seasons in a tiny, walled-in garden. What she looks for most anxiously, the arrival of her long absent lover, almost never occurs. Occasionally, she will visit the garden, which is locked away from the outside world by a series of barred gates, to enjoy the sight of butterflies and song-birds at their carefree pleasures as she walks along precious stepping stones sunk deep in luxuriant moss. The garden may contain, along with its trees and flowering plants, a well—the turning of whose squeaky windlass as a servant draws water often serves as an unwelcome sort of alarm clock in the morning—and a swing (in China, an amusement for young women rather than for small children).

But visits to the garden are only brief interludes, for they merely serve to emphasize her isolation from the world and call her attention to the passage of time. Eventually, she must climb the steps leading back inside. If she is still active as a courtesan, evening finds her at her dressing table, applying her hazy "moth eyebrows" and redoing her hair in one of the elaborate styles such as the "cicada wing" required by late T'ang fashions. Her hair is to be held in place by jeweled hairpins that often slip alluringly loose in the course of the evening's dancing, and she wears jingling pendants of jade hanging from her sash. Her makeup completed, dressed in layers of thin damask or gauze, she takes her place at last as an entertainer at a banquet. Here, much like a Japanese *geisha*, her job is to sing and dance to the accompaniment of pipes (*sheng*, a sort of keyed mouth-organ) or transverse flutes of central Asian origin, play drinking games, and flirt with the guests, giving them what we would call "come-hither" looks, likened in Chinese to ripples on the surface of a limpid autumn pool. When, late at night, the musicians have left and the guests have gone home, the courtesan is left with nothing but the wine-soddened memory of another pointless evening spent entertaining others. She returns to her room, looks for signs of age appearing in her mirror, and lies down on her cold and empty bed, there to pass the rest of the night either sleepless or in happy dreams that soon prove all too brief and unreal.

Many of the images found in these poems recur in a strikingly large percentage of them. Falling flower petals or damaged vegetation appear in more than a quarter of the Feng Yen-ssu poems translated here, fully thirty-four of which are set in the spring; in only seven is there no hint of the season. Such elements as the wind, music, the moon or other heavenly bodies, birds, dreams, and willow trees recur so often in Feng's poems as to be almost more noticeable when they are absent than otherwise. Many actions are repeated in the same way: awakening from sleep or wine, climbing to a high place, leaning against a railing, reflecting on the past, drinking, and the dispersal of a party, to mention only a few of the more prominent. But the very fact that a few pages can supply most of the background needed to understand this large body of verse is bound to raise for modern Western readers, the children of Beethoven and Picasso, grave questions of value. Modern readers may be more puzzled by the esteem that generations of Chinese readers have accorded these works, whose world of physical imagery and sentiment seems so restricted, than by the poems themselves. Members of an age that places a primary value on individuality and originality may feel little interest in a collection of poems almost all of which are written about a very limited number of situations and use a very limited body of conventional imagery. What, such readers may ask, was the point of writing these poems? How can one conclude that some of them are better than others if they all tell more or less the same story and in more or less the same words? It is essential, in order to answer such questions, to realize that the interest of these poems does not lie purely in the description of these languishing beauties and the luxurious furnishings of their chill and lonely boudoirs. Nor is it expected that sympathy for their plight alone will win approbation for the poet. Other elements are at work.

One is the sound of the poems. In common with true lyrics to songs in many cultures, these *tz'u* poems were expected to have a certain quality of mellifluousness or "singability" attained by the use of overlapping phonetic links based on alliteration and vowel harmony. The creation of these and the highlighting of individual words by making them either embody or stand apart from the phonetic texture of the entire poem were important elements in *tz'u* composition. Consider, for example, Li Yü's lyric to "Tzu-yeh Ko" (VIII). The first couplet is dominated by syllables with "muddy" initials (those with an "h"; see the explanation of the transcription below), especially *xh*. In fact, such initials begin eight of its fourteen syllables, compared to only two of the ten in the next couplet. The implicit claim to universal truth of the first line is reinforced by its phonetic homogeneity (e.g., *šeng džhèn xhèn- xhâ nèng*) and the continuation of this into the second line suggests that it too has the same sort of force. *Siau* and *dhok* stand out from the texture of the couplet for emphasis ("I a*lone* so over*whelmed*"). The second couplet works in quite a different way. Instead of a thick, somewhat repetitive texture of similar sounds, it is made up of small units (*kuè- kuk/küi, kyak; mong- drhüong;*

lai/lüi-) that emphasize two syllable phrases, an additional contrast with the first couplet. Note the various links across the stanza break: *kyak/kau*, *lai/lüi-/lĕu, žhüi/žhüi/žhiang-*. They, together with the repetition of the music in performance, would have helped maintain continuity from line to line. The argument of this poem is not, as *tz'u* go, especially disjunct and does not really require the help of a smooth and continuous phonetic texture to keep up its forward motion. Thus it is interesting to find that the lines in the second stanza are linked by the repetition of *-ang: žhiang-; drhiang/ vang-; üang:*. Only the last line fails to join this pattern, but it does something else that is at least equally interesting, which is to begin with *xh-*. This sound has not been heard since the first couplet, in which it was very prominent. Its reappearance thus reinforces what any contemporary would have realized in any case—that the poem is approaching its end, just as the recurrence of *mong-* ("dream") resumes the theme of the entire poem.

In other cases, the handling of phonetic effects is less closely linked to the meaning of the lines. In the seventh of Feng Yen-ssu's poems to the melody "Ts'ai Sang-tzu," for example, their function is simply to smooth the flow of words by numerous overlapping links created by alliteration and vowel harmony. A catalogue of these may make tedious reading, but it should illustrate the point and is worth giving: *šèng, fang-; fang-, san-; san- rin; küi k̦'ĭè- / dhok siok kyang; kyang / ngüat žhiang:; žhiang:, šiu / tšüè; puan-, liam kwa-; kwa- ngüok kèu / k'i:; tiam: kiam:; kiam: kying; kying yiu; tš'ĭè- tš'ĭè-, džhèu / džhèu / bhing drhiang-; bhing drhiang- tong / tsiang; tsiang ts'üè:; li sim; kuâ kyüt*. The density of such phonetic links is not always so great, but many of the other poems in this volume approach it, and some, such as Feng's fourth lyric to "Yeh Chin Men" (XXXIII), surpass it. In other cases, phonetic effects are more local in their workings. For example, in the last two lines of Feng Yen-ssu's second poem to "Ch'üeh T'a Chih," the phonetically similar elements of four corresponding pairs of syllables support the static thematic function of the couplet as a vignette, a "non-answer" to the question put in the preceding line, while the smooth flow of phonetic links in the corresponding lines of the fourth poem underlines its character as a clearly articulated concluding statement. The closing lines of both stanzas of Li Ching's second lyric on "Huan Hsi Sha" are similarly set off phonetically from what precedes them in a way that supports their meaning, while the concluding lines of Li Yü's "Tieh Lien Hua" (XV) owe their isolation not to their own phonetic qualities, but rather to the almost hypnotic repetition of vowel patterns in the sixth and eighth lines of the poems, from which the "rational" coda represents an escape.

It seems quite clear that the kind of phonetic effects we have been considering were not part of the conscious technique of early *tz'u* poets, though of course rhyming and alliterative compounds were well known and apparently as old as the Chinese language itself. Thus each poem presents different features when examined in this light. No large-scale study has yet been devoted to this aspect of the *tz'u*, but there is no doubt much to be discovered.[43] It is with this in mind that I have given a transcription of each lyric along with its translation in this volume.

Equally important is an aspect of the *tz'u* that might be called kinetic; that is, more important than the scene presented by the poem taken as a completed whole is the experience of its parts as they appear in sequence in the performance of the song. These lyrics are as sensual as poetry can be, and they depend for much of their effect upon the reader—intended to be a listener, of course—experiencing one after another the sensations evoked by the text. Vision, hearing, smell, touch, even taste are the matter of many of these poems, as are their rapid shifts of perspective and time, and it is these to which one must be constantly attentive. The Southern T'ang *tz'u* poets are particularly accomplished in their treatment of this aspect of the *tz'u*. In Feng Yen-ssu's tenth lyric to "Ch'üeh T'a Chih," for instance, there is an ambiguous temporal relationship between the stanzas, the scene of the second being perhaps a continuation of the first, a memory of the earlier meetings, or a reflection on the pattern of the singer's life between the earlier meetings and the one referred to in the first stanza. Or, the poem can be read taking the scene of the second stanza as the occasion during which the scene of the first is remembered. The ear is invoked in the second of Feng's "Ts'ai Sang-tzu" poems, in which the sounds in the first and last lines are used to "frame" the poem and give significance to the rest of it. Sounds are used in a similar way in the sixth poem to the same melody, to break off an apparently "pointless" moment of existence. This usage recurs fairly frequently in these poems. While a few of them lead to an explicit conclusion, question, or comment, many seem, as their ends approach, to be drifting into a kind of inertia-bound limbo, from which persona and reader alike are startled by the intrusion of some concrete sensual stimulus. There is, after all, no satisfactory rational conclusion to which the meditations of the personae in these poems can lead. They simply go on until some external force intervenes to break them off. Thus the continual reference to sensual experience is not only a theme of many of the poems, but also a structural device.

But sound and sensuousness do not create significance; they only contribute to it. In the final example, the thirteenth of Feng Yen-ssu's lyrics to the melody "Ch'üeh T'a Chih," it is possible to piece together a reasonably coherent account of the situation to which the poem refers—the forsaken beauty whose sorrow is most acute just as she wakes up after being drunk, making her sob helplessly and then wipe away her teardrop sodden makeup (originally applied in a stylish pattern intended to suggest tearstains), how she stands at her upstairs vantage point staring at the heedless passersby, the high mountains that separate her from her lover, and the blossoms that tumble helplessly at the mercy of a spring breeze. But this picture emerges only in contemplating the poem as a whole. Taken as a sequence of images and impressions, the effect is one of disjunct and uncertain progress, continually delayed or qualified by ironies and discontinuities. The tensions built into the poem are remarkably complex, considering its brevity: the heightened consciousness of the glaring wall and the drip of the clock following on a drunken stupor; the "single dab" of feeling that leads to many dabs of powder stain; the makeup whose pretence of sadness is intended to be charming in public, but which turns to soiling evidence of genuine misery in solitude; the spring emotion (love) that is torment in the first stanza, linked to the east wind (of spring, and thus romance) that continues to blow when there is no longer occasion for it in the second; the irony attached to a breeze that evokes love, but also brings ruin to the blossoms; the repetition of "cold," once as a sensation drawing to an end, then as part of a specific time that is drawing near. The repetition itself is prominent because it occurs at exactly the same place in each stanza, thus transfixing the two separate halves of the poem through a common, but not equivalent, point. Many of these things are conventions themselves, but their density in the poem reflects the need to make sense of a series of discrete and otherwise unrelated images: white wall, dripping clock, sozzled wench, heartbreak, powder-stained dress, blossoms, passersby, letters, eaves, mountains, and hairdress. It is this tension between the apparently random and even irrational sequence of human experience and the overwhelming need of human beings to make conventional sense of it that lies at the heart of the generic meaning of the *tz'u*. Feng Yen-ssu's lyric is "about" the lonely girl who appears in it only in the sense that the "Prague" Symphony is "about" D-major; in each case the work is an experience built around a set of expectations, an experience whose individuality and value lie precisely in the unpredictable, but convincing, twists and turns of presentation that it takes within a system of understood common conventions. Just as the sonata form "means" that conflict and tension are essential elements of human existence, that it is within the power of human beings to resolve them, and that to do so is an occasion for exhilaration and celebration, most of these *tz'u* poems mean that the passage of time is inexorable, that loneliness and remorse are inevitable consequences of it, and that human experience is something fundamentally non-rational and non-moral, something whose anguish is both a consequence of moments of intense emotional or physical sensation and redeemed by them.

Much of this was new to the Chinese poetic tradition, and one might be tempted to suppose that the appearance of such radical pessimism and sensualism was a reaction to the anarchy and violence of contemporary life. But this is so only in the most indirect sense. Just as the emergence of "hard-edge" painting is the result not so much of the psychological alienation of our age as of the discovery of the acrylic paint that makes such painting feasible (though the technological revolution of which the discovery was an incidental part may well have contributed to the alienation), so it may have been the concrete social reality of the time that led the literati poets to take up the *tz'u*. But it was the nature of the form itself that encouraged them to develop it in the way they did. The *tz'u* differed formally from the orthodox *shih* in several respects: the words were to be sung to a melody that was in existence before they were written; the lines were of unequal length; and a stanzaic pattern was often involved. All three of these encouraged poets to explore modes of expression that were not natural to the *shih*. The presence of a familiar melody as an integral part of the completed lyric meant that continuity was in a certain sense guaranteed, freeing the poet to explore possibilities of sudden and unexplained shifts in imagery or tone. The knowledge that the poem was to be "performed" by a stranger whose every characteristic (sex, age, social and economic station, and so forth) was very different from those of the poet allowed the latter to escape from one of the most pervasive assumptions embodied in the Chinese literary tradition—that a literary work ought to reflect more or less faithfully some actual experience or emotion of the poet (indeed, we have seen its pervasiveness here, in the autobiographical interpretations imposed upon Li Yü's lyrics). The uneven lines, as opposed to the tightly organized couplets that were the basic unit of *shih* poetry, similarly encouraged the exploitation of assymetrical balances and the treatment of individual lines as independent entities. The division of many of the common *tz'u* melodies into two stanzas encouraged a break in the verbal continuity midway through the poem, in contrast to the tendency of T'ang *shih* to divide into three sections.[44] Indeed, the handling of the two stanzas is often an important formal aspect of individual *tz'u* poems, for the tendency of the stanzas (like the two halves of a painted folding screen) to present complementary views of the same subject had to be balanced against the interest in a continuous, "durchkomponiert" structure. In some cases, such as Li Yü's lyrics to "Wang Chiang-nan" and "Wang Chiang Mei," the contrast between the stanzas is so complete that they are really separate poems. In others, the shift in perspective is one of the most important features of the poem as a unified whole, often in conjunction with some element that is common to both halves, such as the "cold" in the Feng Yen-ssu poem. To return to a musical analogy, the "redness" of Li Yü's "Yi Hu Chu," and the obsessive concentration of the poem on the mouth of the tipsy singer, for example, function in a way similar to the presence of a second 'cello in Schubert's Quintet in C or the basset horns in the Mozart Requiem. They characterize the entire work and contribute to its continuity, but their very pervasiveness excludes them from use as a basis for the structure of the whole. By contrast, the shift from the pert control of the first stanza of Li's poem to the sloppy, drunken, "aslant" quality of the second is fundamental to the meaning of the poem, just as the resolution of the flat second in the last two notes of the Schubert or the repetition of the Kyrie fugue in the Requiem (whether the work of Mozart or of Süssmayr) could not be altered without changing the meaning of the entire work.

It was their greater mastery of this kind of complex interplay between literal and structural meaning that made the works of the Southern T'ang lyric poets, especially Feng Yen-ssu, so important for the later development of the form. As Yeh Chia-ying has remarked, Feng's lyrics represent the most important historical development in the *tz'u* of the ninth century, while those of Li Yü are a kind of extra-historical phenomenon.[45] The particular importance of Feng Yen-ssu may be owing in part to accidental causes connected with the way in which his collected lyrics were edited. In any event, his *oeuvre* is much more homogeneous, both in style and in quality. The consistency and availability of his work, which, if it does not often rise to the level of Li's finest lyrics, at least never falls to the level of the latter's "Ch'ang Hsiang Ssu," may have made it a particularly potent force in the development of the lyric. Although a number of early Sung lyric poets are stylistically almost indistinguishable from Feng Yen-ssu, the closest thing to a successful imitation of Li Yü does not appear until the Manchu poet Singde, in the seventeenth century. It was at least a century after the fall of Southern T'ang before the *tz'u* came to be accepted as a fully "respectable" literary form by the Sung literati, who had revived for their class the public role first evolved by the scholar-officials of the eighth and early ninth centuries. But from the very first years of the Sung, there were writers (too eminent or too obscure to concern themselves overmuch with respectability) who devoted their energies to developing and exploiting the new possibilities that the form offered. Without the example of the Southern T'ang poets, it is quite possible that they would not have done so.[46]

Almost the entire literary production of the Southern T'ang court has been lost. The "complete works" of only two of its writers—Li Chien-hsün and Hsü Hsüan—have been preserved.[47] Of Li Yü's collected works in the orthodox forms, originally in thirty books, less than twenty *shih* poems survive, along with about a dozen pieces of prose, only a few of which are of any interest as literature. Of Li Ching's work we have even less: two *shih* poems and some scattered prose. And by Feng Yen-ssu, one *shih* and two prose pieces. So far as we know, there was never a Southern T'ang *tz'u* anthology corresponding to the *Hua-chien Chi* in Shu, although a number of lyrics by Feng Yen-ssu and Li Yü, as well as others by a variety of early *tz'u* poets, were collected in the eleventh century anthology *Tsun-ch'ien Chi* ("Beside the Winecups"). Thus we have a much smaller body of surviving verse from the southern state than from the western one. A collection of Feng Yen-ssu's lyrics was printed in 1058, and it appears likely that the current editions of *Yang-ch'un Chi* derive from it. It is unlikely that any of Li Yü's *tz'u* were included in his collected works. In the first place, it was only later that the *tz'u* became sufficiently established to claim a place in most writers' collected editions.[48] In the second, the compilation of the *Nan-T'ang Erh-chu Tz'u* seems to have been done from scratch. This would not have been necessary had the *tz'u* been included in Li's regular collection, which probably survived at least until 1300 or so, since it is cited in the critical anthology *Ying-k'uei Lü-sui*, compiled by Fang Hui (1227–1306).[49]

The *Nan-T'ang Erh-chu Tz'u* is a much smaller and, at first sight, a more haphazard collection than the *Yang-ch'un Chi*. The questions surrounding its compilation and the genealogy of the various extant editions are sufficiently complicated that I intend to deal with them separately elsewhere.[50] The facts of interest to us here have been established by the early Republican period scholar Wang Kuo-wei and by Wang Chung-wen. The collection appears to have been edited in a bookshop as a commercial venture, since the poems appear in groups according to the sources from which they were copied. The most likely period for this to have been done is 1167–73. There is a reference to "The Lyric Poems of Li Yü" (*Li Hou-chu Tz'u*) in a bibliography compiled by a man who died in 1194, so at the very least it is certain that some collection of the poems existed by then,[51] and there is no real reason to suppose that it was not the ancestor of the ones current today. A somewhat later bibliography, probably compiled in the 1230's, records the present title for the first time and gives a brief description of the book that closely matches the extant texts.[52]

As one would perhaps expect, given the long interval that elapsed between the composition of the poems and their publication, the individual pieces in both the *Yang-ch'un Chi* and the *Nan-T'ang Erh-chu Tz'u* present numerous problems of authenticity. Most of the problems in *Yang-ch'un Chi* are of one of two kinds. First, some of the poems are also found in the *Hua-chien Chi*, attributed there to a variety of poets. These poems are probably not by Feng at all, for, although he was old enough to have written them by the time of the compilation of the *Hua-chien Chi* in 940, the editors of the latter work were apparently personally acquainted with most of the contemporary poets whose work was included, and it seems unlikely that they would have unwittingly incorporated verses by a young man from a different kingdom. More problematic by far are those poems that are also attributed to poets of the Northern Sung, chiefly to Ou-yang Hsiu (1007–72). Here the evidence is complex and often inconclusive, but I tend to accept Feng's authorship of these poems as a group, in part because a few of them rhyme according to categories that match Feng's practice, but not that of Ou-yang. The compilation of the *Nan-T'ang Erh-chu Tz'u* seems to have been fairly carefully done; only one positively spurious poem (IX) was included, original sources were noted, a number of privately owned manuscripts were consulted, and, perhaps as a result, only a few apparently genuine poems still in existence were omitted. On the other hand, a poem by the Yuan dynasty poet and dramatist Pai P'u (1226–85), whose subtitle tells us that he assembled it from lines and expressions found in various *tz'u* by Li Yü, contains many phrases not found in Li's surviving lyrics.[53] Pai P'u was active in the North at a time when all communication with Southern Sung was cut off. So it may be that there was a fuller, or at least a different, collection of Li's *tz'u* available in the North, one that has since been lost.

For the present volume I have limited my choice among the lyrics of Feng Yen-ssu to those poems about whose authenticity I feel no serious doubts. In the case of the *Nan-T'ang Erh-chu Tz'u*, however, I have excluded only the one poem that can be shown without doubt to be a misattribution. I have, moreover, added four uncollected but probably genuine lyrics by Li Yü at the end. Appendix A consists of the few surviving *shih* poems of Feng Yen-ssu, Li Ching, and Li Yü, and two pieces of the latter's prose, including the "Dirge for Empress Chao-hui." The *shih* poems are universally ignored, and I would certainly not want to claim for them anything like the importance of the *tz'u*. Nonetheless, some of them are quite attractive, and they do add to an understanding of the poets. In Appendix B, I translate a group of lyrics that are definitely spurious, but so often taken to be genuine in popular works that they now form a kind of unofficial supplement to the proper collection.

The transcription of these poems is based on the reconstruction of Late Middle Chinese (LMC) by E. G. Pulleyblank (see his "Late Middle Chinese"). I have modified this system in a number of respects. Some changes have been made simply for typographical convenience or ease of reading by non-linguists; others reflect differences between the ninth-century northern dialect that is the basis of LMC and the tenth-century southern language of Li Yü. Evidence in support of the latter sort of change is given in my article on rhyming categories. In addition, certain changes that are not reflected in rhyming are assumed to have taken place by the time of Li Yü, notably those given below under numbers A.3, B.2, B.3, B.4, and C.8. Since literary scholars are often understandably wary of the intricacies of historical phonology, it may be helpful to give an account here of how the transcription was arrived at, especially since much of the explanation will apply to later T'ang and Sung poetry in general. This is followed by a guide to its pronunciation intended to be useful to readers without linguistic background.

The essential reference required is the *Kuang-yün Sheng-hsi* of Shen Chien-shih, which should be checked against Liang Seng-pao's *Ssu-sheng Yün-p'u*. For each character (or each reading, in the case of characters that have multiple readings), Shen gives four items of information: 1) the initial, which is to be read according to the table in Pulleyblank, p. 210; 2) the *Kuang-yün* rhyme, which is converted to a rhyme group (*she* 攝) by reference to Liang Seng-pao and then transcribed as in Pulleyblank, p. 236; 3) an indication that the reading is either 開 "open," or 合 "closed"; and 4) the "grade" (*teng* 等), represented by a number from one to four. The latter two indications supply the medial of the syllable, which can be transcribed according to the table in Pulleyblank, p. 231.

Once the basic transcription has been done according to this procedure, it can be simplified as suggested in Pulleyblank, p. 145. Additional modifications are as follows (references to supporting evidence are to Pulleyblank "LMC" or to my study of rhyming ["Rhyming"]; modifications made simply as a matter of typographical convenience, implying no change in actual pronunciation, are labelled "graph"):

A. INITIALS

1. "Muddy" initials are written as voiced (rather than unvoiced, as in Pulleyblank) consonants followed by *h* (graph): *kh>gh, th>dh, ph>bh*, etc.; note that *xh* is unchanged.
2. The glottal stop is written as a period (graph): 安 *.an*
3. Labial initials followed by closed third grade medials (*iu* or *y*, here *ü*) become dentilabial fricatives ("LMC," pp. 216–19, 231): *p>f, p'>f, ph>bh>vh, m>v*
4. The two retroflex initials 牀 (*džh-*) and 禪 (*žh-*) were confused in the early rhyme tables; they are both treated here as *džh-* in second grade syllables and as *žh-* in third ("LMC," pp. 222–24).

B. MEDIALS

1. Medials *-j-* and *-y-* (or *-iu-*) are here *-y-* and *-ü-* (graph).
2. After labial initials (*p, p', bh, m*), the open second grade medial *-y-* is lost ("LMC," pp. 128–31): 巴 *pya>pa*
3. In rhyme Group VI (*-au*), open first grade syllables after labial initials have a medial *-u-* ("LMC," pp. 167–68): 寶 *pau:>puau:*
4. In rhyme Group XI (*-ang*), second grade syllables with retroflex affricate or fricative initials acquire a medial *-w-* ("LMC," p. 123): 莊 *tšang>tšwang*
5. Shen Chien-shih and Liang Seng-pao are confusing in their treatment of certain syllables in rhyme Group XII (*-ong*). Shen is to be followed with the following exceptions ("LMC," pp. 126–27, 128):

a) syllables from the *Kuang-yün* rhyme 冬 , which Shen lists as "closed first grade" (implying *-uong*), should be transcribed as open (*-ong*).

b) syllables in the *Kuang-yün* rhyme 東 in third grade with labial stop initials had shifted to closed at an early stage, and so their initials become fricatives in the regular way. E.g. 風 *piong>püong>fung*.

c) syllables corresponding to the preceding but with the labial initial *m-* did not undergo this change, but do shift to first grade. E.g. 夢 *miong->mong-*; 目 *miok>mok*. (Liang Seng-pao treats these syllables as closed fourth grade, implying *myüong-*, etc.).

C. FINALS

1. The basic forms are as follows (graph):

I. -â	V. -i	IX. -êng	XIII. -an
II. -a	VI. -au	X. -êng	XIV. -ên
III. -ê	VII. -êu	XI. -ang	XV. -am
IV. -ai	VIII. -ang	XII. -ong	XVI. -êm

2. Groups I and II are kept distinct in Southern T'ang rhyming, rather than being lumped together as in LMC ("LMC," pp. 238–39; "Rhyming," Tables I-III). My *â* was phonetically probably /ɔ/.

3. Group IV syllables in second grade in level and departing tones with velar or throat initials (in rhymes 佳, 卦 , and 夬 *only*) lose their final *-i* ("Rhyming," Table XVII): 佳 *kyai>kya* 卦 *kwai->kwa-*; also 罷 *bhyai->bhai->bha-*; but 隘 *kyai*, 解 *kyai:*

4. Group IV syllables in third and fourth grade merge with Group V ("Rhyming," Tables VII-VIII): *siai->si-* *kyüai>kyüi*

5. Syllables originally in Group V (that is, *not* those governed by the preceding section) in grades II and IV, open, with retroflex or dental sibilant initials change their vowel from *-i* to *i* ("LMC," p. 236): *džhi>žhi* *si>si* *si>si*

6. Groups VIII and XI merge as *-ang* ("Rhyming," Tables X-XIV).

7. Groups IX and X also merge, as *-êng* ("Rhyming," Tables XV-XVI). The general loss of *-ê-* after tense vowels (*i, i, u, ü*) and before a consonant or semivowel (i.e. in open third and fourth grades and closed first, third, and fourth in Groups V, VII, IX, XIV, and XVI, see "LMC," p. 145) extends to Group X following this merger: *dhiêng>dhing* *tšiêng>tšing:*

In addition, open second grade syllables with throat initials shift to fourth grade: *xhyêng>xhying* *.yêng>.ying*

8. In Group XIII (*-an*), Southern T'ang poets rhyme first and second grade syllables separately from third and fourth grades in level tone only. The distinction was probably similar to that found in modern Mandarin between

a more open -*a* in first and second grades and a closer vowel /ε/ in third and fourth ("Rhyming," Table V): 干 *kan* 間 *kyan* 健 *ghian-* 見 *kyian-*; but 言 *ngien*

9. Rising tone syllables with muddy initials shift to departing tone ("LMC," p. 141): 斷 *dhuan:>dhuan-*

10. Two irregular words: 不 *put* 否 *fu:*

If the reconstruction is a complicated matter to prepare, it is fortunately not especially difficult to pronounce once it has been written down. A Chinese syllable can be broken down into three parts: initial, medial, and final. Not every syllable has all three, but all have a final. In *drhiang-*, for example, *drh* is the initial, *i* the medial, and *ang-* the final. *Tang* has no medial, and *yiang* no initial. This much being said, let us look at the individual consonant and vowel sounds that were used in the syllables of Southern T'ang Chinese. There are only six consonants that can come at the end of a syllable: *ng, n, m, k, t,* and *p,* and all of these are pronounced essentially as they would be at the end of an English word. Initial consonants are somewhat more complicated, and definitely more numerous, so it will perhaps be easier to present them in tabular form:

unaspirated stops and affricates	*k*	*t*	*tr*	*p*	*ts*	*tš*	.
aspirated stops	*k'*	*t'*	*tr'*	*p'*	*ts'*	*tš'*	*x*
"muddy" stops and affricates	*gh*	*dh*	*drh*	*bh*	*dzh*	*džh*	
voiceless fricatives				*f*	*s*	*š*	
voiced fricatives				*v*			
"muddy" fricatives				*vh*	*zh*	*žh*	*xh*
nasals	*ng*	*n*	*nr*	*m*			
laterals				*l*		*r*	

Now, most of these can be pronounced as in English, but a few present special problems. The most important of these is the meaning of "muddy," which refers to a voiced aspiration that gives a breathy quality to the entire syllable. The difference between aspirated and unaspirated stops exists in English, but we do not use it to tell words apart, and so most native speakers are unaware of it. The difference between *t* and *t'*, for example, is that between the t's of *stop* and *top*. The only other consonants likely to be at all puzzling are *x, xh,* ., and those that include *š* or *ž*. *X* is simply English *h,* as in *home,* spelt with an *x* to keep it distinct from the "muddy" sounds. *Xh* is then a muddy *h.* A period occurring at the beginning of a syllable stands for the glottal stop, the sound that comes before the vowel in "Ann!". The column with *š* and *ž* is easier to pronounce than to explain. The sound of *š* is essentially that of the *sh* in "shrill," with the tongue sharply curled back at the tip. A *ch,* as in "Charlie," pronounced with the tongue in this position is a good approximation for *tš'*, and the other sounds in the column can be arrived at by analogy.

Vowels and semivowels present very few problems:

â as in *au*thor	*o* as in b*oo*k	*y* as in *y*odel
a as in f*a*ther	*u* as in r*u*de	*ê* as in sof*a*
i as in sk*i*	*ü* as in t*u* or *ü*ber	*w* as in s*w*ami
i̵ something like s*u*ppose		
ai as in m*y*		
au as in l*ou*d		
ều something like l*ow*		

One important feature of the language that we cannot reconstruct with any certainty, though we know it existed, is its tonal quality. We do know that there were four tonal classes, but we cannot be sure how they sounded, except that the fourth of them (entering), distinguished by the final consonants -*p*, -*t*, and -*k*, was probably quite short and abrupt. Since this tone was treated in prosody as equivalent to the second (rising) and third (departing) tones, in opposition to the first (level), it seems likely that the level tone was longer than the others. In the transcription used here, the rising and departing tones are marked with : and - respectively. The entering tone is distinguished by its final consonants, and all other unmarked syllables are in level tone.

NOTES

1. His name is occasionally misread as Yen-chi 己, as in A. R. Davis, ed., *The Penguin Book of Chinese Verse*, pp. xx, 34, 83, and Michael Workman, "The Bedchamber *Topos* in the *Tz'u* Songs of Three Medieval Chinese Poets: Wen T'ing-yün, Wei Chuang, and Li Yü." See Hsia Ch'eng-t'ao, "Feng Cheng-chung Nien-p'u," p. 35, for an explanation of the correct reading.

2. Here I summarize in the briefest and simplest way what was in actuality a very complex historical process, one that had profound effects on Chinese society for many years after. The best concise introduction to T'ang history is probably the "Introduction" to Wright and Twitchett's *Perspectives on the T'ang*. See also Jacques Gernet, *Le Monde Chinois*, esp. pp. 228–306, 638–46. For an account of the problems posed by provincial military autonomy after the An Lu-shan Rebellion and of the most successful attempt to solve them, see Charles A. Peterson, "The Restoration Completed." Denis Twitchett, in "Varied Patterns of Provincial Autonomy," has discussed the nature of decentralized authority in the later T'ang period and the particular conditions that led to stability and prosperity in the Yangtse region that eventually became the territory of Wu and Southern T'ang. For an annotated translation of the standard account of Huang Ch'ao in the *Hsin T'ang Shu*, together with pertinent material from Arabic sources, see Howard Levy, *Biography of Huang Ch'ao*. For a detailed account of the reunification of the North, see Wang Gungwu, *The Structure of Power in North China During the Five Dynasties*. A more recent study by Wang, "The Middle Yangtse in T'ang Politics," does a great deal to clarify the nature of Southern T'ang's opportunities and failures on its western frontier. Wang does, incidentally, misread Li Pian's name, 昇, as "Sheng" 昪 on pp. 231, 449. Since this was drafted, the first of two volumes of the Cambridge History of China to be devoted to the Sui and T'ang dynasties has appeared with a much fuller account of T'ang political history than had been available in any Western language previously.

3. Kung Ying-tê examines the evidence relating to "Li Pien's" ancestry and concludes that Li was not related to the T'ang royal house at all ("Nan-T'ang Tsu-shih K'ao-lüeh"). Hsia Ch'eng-t'ao comes to the same conclusion ("Nan-T'ang Erh-chu Nien-p'u," pp. 73–74).

4. See Hsia Ch'eng-t'ao, "Nan-T'ang," p. 94, for a discussion of Li Ching's succession. The story cited here comes from a collection of anecdotes, the *Wu-kuo Ku-shih* (A.7ab) that is not entirely reliable; cf. the biography of Ching-ta in Lu Yu, *Nan-T'ang Shu*, 16.6a–7b. Perhaps the main point here is not what actually happened, but what people were prepared to believe had happened.

5. Hsia Ch'eng-t'ao, "Feng Cheng-chung," p. 37; Lin Wen-pao, *Feng Yen-ssu Yen-chiu*, pp. 17–47.

6. The personal name of the author, who claims to be recording and commenting on material received from his father, is unknown. See Lin Wen-pao, pp. 17–18.

7. Lin Wen-pao, pp. 18–26, 34–35.

8. See Hsia Ch'eng-t'ao, "Feng Cheng-chung," pp. 59–60, for a discussion of this anecdote, and Lin Wen-pao, pp. 41–45, for Feng's relationship with Sun Sheng. The source for Feng's comment is Wen-ying, *Yü-hu Ch'ing-hua*, 10.7b.

9. For this speech, see Lu Yu, *Nan-T'ang Shu*, 11.1ab, and Hsia Ch'eng-t'ao, "Feng Cheng-chung," pp. 46–47.

NOTES

10. Lin Wen-pao, pp. 4–5, cites and disagrees with an example of this, from Ch'en T'ing-cho's *Pai-yü Chai Tz'u-hua*, 5.14b–15a (rpt. pp. 3922–23).

11. It should be noted—with the accusation that he was responsible for Southern T'ang's expansionist programme in mind—that Feng was not Chief Minister when the invasions of Min and Ch'u were launched. That he was brought in after they were under way and encountering difficulties suggests that he may have been more moderating in his influence and capable in administration than has been generally recognized.

12. There are two useful surveys of high culture in Southern T'ang, an old one in Japanese by Naba Toshisada, "Kankaseraretaru Nan-Tō Bunka no Kachi," and a more recent one in Chinese by Lin Jui-han, "Nan-T'ang chih Ching-chi yü Wen-hua." Murakami Tetsumi (*Ri Iku*, pp. 8–11) also points out the importance of Southern T'ang's relative cultural superiority to the North. For a monographic treatment of one of the most important Southern T'ang painters, see Richard Barnhart, *Marriage of the Lord of the River*. Many more are treated briefly in Alexander Soper, *Kuo Jo-hsü's Experiences in Painting*, passim. I have prepared a study of the position occupied by two Southern T'ang landscapists in succeeding periods, "The Landscape Painters Tung Yuan and Chü-jan in Sung Dynasty Literature."

13. Tung Shih, *Huang-Sung Shu-lu*, B.1a. For additional comments on Li's calligraphy and a listing of his work in the imperial collection ca. 1120, see *Hsüan-ho Shu-p'u*, 12.1a–2b.

14. See her biographies in Ma Ling, *Nan-T'ang Shu*, 6.3b–8a, including Li's "Dirge" (translated in Appendix A), and Lu Yü, *Nan-T'ang Shu, 16.2-b–3b*.

15. Ma Ling, *Nan-T'ang Shu*, 6.4ab.

16. Lu Yu, *Nan-T'ang Shu*, 16.3b. Lu appends this story to his account of Chao-hui, introducing it with the words, "someone says."

17. Kunichi Minoru discusses the role of Buddhism in Li Yü's life and works in "Ri Iku no Shōgai," pp. 14–23.

18. See R. H. van Gulik, *Sexual Life in Ancient China*, p. 216, and Howard Levy, *Chinese Footbinding*, pp. 38–40, for a summary of Chinese accounts of Li Yü's connection with the origins of footbinding. Van Gulik does express some scepticism in this regard.

19. See Kuo Te-hao, "Li Hou-chu P'ing-chuan," p. 161, for the story. The source is quite late, the *Tzu-pu-yü* ("What Confucius Didn't Say") of the eighteenth-century poet and man of letters Yuan Mei (9.7a–8a [5569]). On this collection, see Arthur Waley, *Yuan Mei*, pp. 120–40.

20. Hsia Ch'eng-t'ao ("Nan-T'ang Erh-chu Nien-p'u," p. 126) quotes the *Hao-jan Chai Ya-t'an* of Chou Mi, which in turn quotes a book called the *Tao-shan Hsin-wen* (*Hao-jan Chai Ya-t'an*, B.9ab). The *Hao-jan Chai Ya-t'an* itself was lost, but it has been reconstructed on the basis of quotations in the *Yung-lo Ta-tien* encyclopedia (see Hsia Ch'eng-t'ao, "Chou Ts'ao-ch'uang Nien-p'u," p. 372; Hsia concludes that the book must have been compiled between the fall of the Southern Sung in 1279 and Chou Mi's death in 1298). The same passage is quoted in the *Ch'o-keng Lu* of T'ao Tsung-yi (10.13ab). For T'ao (ca.1316–ca.1402), see L. Carrington Goodrich and Chaoying Fang, eds., *Dictionary of Ming Biography, 1368–1644*, pp. 1268–72, where the date of the *Ch'o-keng Lu* is given as 1366. The *Tao-shan Hsin-wen* was listed in the monograph on bibliography in the *Sung Shih* (206.5231), but is apparently no longer extant. It may be the same work as the *Tao-shan Ch'ing-hua*, which does survive. The latter work is discussed in the *Ssu-k'u Ch'üan-shu Tsung-mu T'i-yao* (pp. 2915–16), whose editors record a number of careless errors in it and also establish the approximate date of its compilation. Yü Chia-hsi discusses the *Tao-shan Ch'ing-hua* at some length (*Ssu-k'u T'i-yao Pien-cheng*, pp. 1066–⁷¹) and proposes, among much else, that it is in fact the same book as the *Hsin-wen* and that it wa com-

piled by someone who had served in the Imperial Library. No reference to footbinding is to be found in extant texts of the *Tao-shan Ch'ing-hua*. Howard Levy gives Chang Pang-chi, rather than Chou Mi, as the source for the anecdote (*Chinese Footbinding*, p. 39), but in fact this is apparently the result of a misreading of the *Ch'o-keng Lu*, in which Chang Pang-chi is quoted first, on the early history of footbinding, followed by the anecdote from the *Tao-shan Hsin-wen*. The latter quotation is not included in T'ao Tsung-yi's source, Chang Pang-chi's *Mo-chuang Man-lu* (8.4b–5a). It may be significant that Chang does not mention Li Yü in this account, but in any event, it is important to correct Levy here, because doing so leaves the *Tao-shan Hsin-wen* as the only source for the story about Li Yü and his consort (an important early Japanese secondary source also cited by Levy, Naka Michiyo's "Shina Fujin Tensoku no Kigen," has the quotations properly separated). An additional reason for doubting the reliability of the original anecdote, or at least the care of the *Tao-shan Hsin-wen*'s compiler, is its citation as part of the entry of a couplet from a poem by one T'ang Hao, which supposedly refers to the dancer on her lotus stage. But T'ang was the official who had recommended that Li Ching move his capital to Yü-chang and later committed suicide to escape punishment when Li began to regret the move, and this means that he was no longer alive during Li Yü's reign, during which the incident is supposed to have occurred.

21. Wang Chih, *Mo-chi*, C.6a.

22. See Yeh Meng-te, *Shih-lin Yen-yü Pien*, quoted in *Ch'üan T'ang Shih*, p. 89; *Sung Shih*, 478.13862; and Wang Chih, *Mo-chi*.

23. Juan T'ing-cho, "Li Yü chih Ssu." See also Hsia Ch'eng-t'ao, "Nan-T'ang Erh-chu Nien-p'u," pp. 155–58. Note that Wang Chih's *Mo-chi*, cited in the two preceding notes, is called into question by Juan.

24. Chou Tsu-chuan expresses reservations about the literal interpretation of the "P'u-sa Man" poems as historical documents (*Sui T'ang Wu-tai Wen-hsüeh Shih*, p. 214), although he seems prepared to accept many of the traditional assignments of the lyrics to particular periods of Li Yü's life. He does note that the "late" poems developed from the "early" ones, rather than being a wholly new departure. One obvious consequence of a proper scepticism concerning such anecdotes as these is that Howard Levy's inference that Hsiao-Chou did not have bound feet (*Chinese Footbinding*, pp. 40, 304 n.16) is unwarranted.

25. Kung Ying-te, "Li Hou-chu Wang-kuo Shih-tz'u Pien-cheng," pp. 93–95. The earliest writer known to me to have doubted the attribution of poem XXXVI to Li Yü is Yuan Wen (1119–90), although he does not raise any doubts about the authenticity of the *Tung-p'o Chih-lin* (*Weng-yu Hsien-p'ing*, 5.8b). Wang Chung-wen (p. 88) finds Yuan's interpretation forced, remarking that he does not escape "glueing the pegs to keep the lute in tune."

26. The most common words in the *Nan-T'ang Erh-chu Tz'u* (including the four additional poems appended to the collection here) are "spring" 春, which occurs twenty-seven times, "one" 一, "blossom" 花, "dream"夢, and "not" 不 (20 each), "person" 人 (19), and "wind" 風 and "moon" 月 (18 each). Of these, only "one" occurs in poem XXXVI. 40.3 per cent of the vocabulary of this poem is found nowhere else in the collection. The next highest such percentage is 36.8 per cent, for poem VII, followed by 31.8 for XXIX. The highest among the Feng Yen-ssu poems selected for this volume is 28.3 per cent, for poem IX. Note, however, that the total size of the two bodies of verse differs—1773 words in the Li Ching and Li Yü poems against 2535 for Feng Yen-ssu's. Thus the chances of any one word's occurring only once are less in the second collection and the percentages not strictly comparable. For additional remarks on comparative vocabulary, see below, note 40.

27. James J. Y. Liu briefly characterizes some differences between *shih* and *tz'u* in his "Some Literary Qualities of the Lyric (*Tz'u*)." See also Shuen-fu Lin, *The Transformation of the Chinese Lyrical Tradition: Chiang K'uei and Southern Sung Tz'u Poetry*, esp. pp. 94–141, and Kang-i

NOTES

Sun Chang, *The Evolution of Chinese* Tz'u *Poetry*, pp. 2–5, 51–58, 169–84.

28. It is true that translators of longer *shih* into Western languages often use a stanza break as a convention to represent a change in rhyme in the Chinese text, but the stanzaic quality is weak or absent in the original.

29. Murakami, (*Ri Iku*, pp. 14–19) gives a concise account of the history of the *tz'u* down to the time of Li Yü. There is an extended, if inconclusive, review of the various theories about the origins of the *tz'u* in Mizuhara Ikō, "Nan-Tō Goshu Shi no Kenkyū," Pt. 1, pp. 16–21 and Pt. 2, pp. 33–37. The best discussion in English is probably still Glen Baxter's "Metrical Origins of the Tz'u," which does not, however, take the materials recovered at Tun-huang much into account. Shih-chuan Chen presents a good deal of additional evidence in two more recent articles, "Dates of Some of the Tunhuang Lyrics" and "The Rise of the Tz'u Reconsidered," but the evidence itself, though it requires the modification of some of Baxter's interpretations, is handled rather badly by Chen, whose uncritical treatment of it and faulty reasoning call some of the conclusions reached into question. A more balanced account than either Baxter or Chen, although earlier than both, is Liu Yün-hsiang, "Wu-ko yü Tz'u."

30. For a study of one of the most influential early figures in the *kung-t'i* tradition, see John Marney, *Liang Chien-wen Ti*.

31. See Liu Yün-hsiang, "Wu-ko yü Tz'u." For an introduction to the Tzu-yeh tradition and a fair-sized body of translations from it—neither, unfortunately, very reliable—see William McNaughton and Lenore Mayhew, *A Gold Orchid*.

32. Some courtesans of the later T'ang were poets in their own right. The most important of these was probably Yü Hsüan-chi, about fifty of whose poems survive. See Jan W. Walls, "The Poetry of Yü Hsüan-chi." There is also a popular account, highly unreliable: Genevieve Wimsatt, *Selling Wilted Peonies*. Note that Yü Hsüan-chi was acquainted with Wen T'ing-yün.

33. For these popular *tz'u*, see Jen Erh-pei, *Tun-huang Ch'ü Ch'u-t'an*, and *Tun-huang Ch'ü Chiao-lu*; also Shih-chuan Chen, "Dates of Some of the Tunhuang Lyrics," and Kang-i Sun Chang, *Evolution*, pp. 15–25.

34. The Li Po poems in particular have been much discussed, and a variety of evidence has been advanced on both sides of the question. Kang-i Sun Chang seems to have been the first to realize that a distinction is to be made between two questions hitherto treated as one (*Evolution*, p. 7). First, could Li Po have written poems to the melodies in question (i.e., were they known in his day)? And second, are the extant poems by him? In fact, as I demonstrate in an unpublished article ("Textual Notes on Some of the Sources for Southern T'ang Tz'u Poetry"), rhyming evidence shows quite conclusively that only three of the poems, the ones that are formally little different from *shih* and whose authenticity has never been seriously questioned, can possibly have been composed earlier than the middle of the tenth century. The rest date from around the year 1000.

35. Aoyama Hiroshi, *Kakanshū Sakuin*, p. ii, no. 017.

36. See, for a typical example, Liu Yün-hsiang, "Wu-ko yü Tz'u," p. 132.

37. This thesis is associated with the late Ch'en Yin-kô, who first advanced it. It is more fully developed in E. G. Pulleyblank, *Background of the Rebellion of An Lu-shan*. There is a brief review of more recent treatments of it in the bibliographical note to Denis Twitchett's "Composition of the T'ang Ruling Class," pp. 83–84.

38. For the problems and prospects facing a young literatus of the late ninth century, see William

H. Nienhauser, Jr., *P'i Jih-hsiu*, pp. 15–37. Note in particular (p. 26) that P'i went first to look for a provincial patron, before attempting the capital examination. Hans Frankel refers to this phenomenon in passing in his "T'ang Literati; A Composite Biography," p. 70. Frankel's entire article is an excellent introduction to the conventions of Chinese biography as applied to T'ang literary figures.

39. For Ts'en Shen, see Wen Yi-to, "Ts'en Chia-chou Hsi-nien K'ao-cheng"; Arthur Waley, "A Chinese Poet in Central Asia"; Marie Chan, "The Frontier Poems of Ts'en Shen"; and Wu-chi Liu and Irving Lo, eds., *Sunflower Splendor*, pp. 143–49, 558–59.

40. There is evidence of the different stylistic preoccupations of the *Hua-chien* and Southern T'ang poets also in their vocabularies. While they have in common an emphasis on some words (flowers, spring, wind), the decorative interest of the *Hua-chien* lyrics is evident in their much more frequent use of such words as incense, jade, halcyon, gold, and pink, while the often more sombre and introspective Southern T'ang poets make greater use of words such as cold, night, rain, and dream. Of course, these are statistical trends rather than absolute diagnostic features, and they need to be qualified in several ways. For one thing, Li Yü and Feng Yen-ssu differ considerably in their usage too. Feng uses "outdoor" (wind, rain, evening, night) and architectural (pavilion, lamp, window, blinds) words much more frequently than does Li Yü, whose emphasis is more explicitly directed toward emotional experience (single, sorrow, regret, dream). Too, as Lin Wen-pao has pointed out, Feng Yen-ssu is distinguished from the *Hua-chien* poets by the greater range of his vocabulary, perhaps a more important index than frequency of particular words.

41. Aoyama Hiroshi, *Kakanshū Sakuin*, p. xviii, no. 246.

42. For a concise outline, see Michael Workman, "The Bedchamber *Topos*." An excellent study by Obi Kōichi, "Nan-Tō no Shi to Shizen," explores the relationship between mood and natural imagery in the Southern T'ang *tz'u* poets.

43. I explore this aspect of Li Yü's lyrics X and XXX–XXXV in considerable detail in my essay, "The Hsieh Hsin En Fragments."

44. See Stephen Owen, *Poetry of the Early T'ang*, pp. 9–11, for a brief outline of "tripartite form," his term for the common *shih* formula of: 1) the introduction of a topic; 2) the amplification of this; and 3) a comment or response. The second of these occupied two couplets of a regulated verse poem; the others, one each. An alternative model is to see the four couplets (or the four lines of a quatrain) as making up four units. These are known, in traditional Chinese criticism, as *ch'i* ("start"), *ch'eng* ("accept," "take up"), *chuan* ("turn"), and *ho* ("unite").

45. Yeh Chia-ying, "Ts'ung *Jen-chien Tz'u-hua*," pp. 139–43. Yeh, pp. 117–43, and Chan An-t'ai, *Li Ching Li Yü Tz'u*, pp. 31–48, are among the best of many accounts of Li's style. That of Li Ching is discussed by Hsieh Shih-ya, "Lun Nan-T'ang Chung-chu Li Ching Tz'u." For that of Feng Yen-ssu, see Cheng Ch'ien, "Lun Feng Yen-ssu Tz'u," Yeh Chia-ying, pp. 91–116, and Lin Wen-pao, pp. 71–98.

46. For an informative and reliable introduction to the more important early Sung *tz'u* poets, see James J. Y. Liu, *Major Lyricists of the Northern Sung*. One critic who does see an influence from Li Yü on early Sung *tz'u* is Mizuhara Ikō, "Nan-Tō Goshu," Pt. 1, pp. 29–31.

47. Among writers not part of the court, only Li Chung and Ch'en T'ao (whose dates are uncertain) are represented by extant collections. In the case of Li Chien-hsün, only the poems are preserved. T'ang Kuei-chang has recently published an annotated listing of all the books known to have been produced in Southern T'ang, "Nan-T'ang Yi-wen Chih." Of a total of 175 titles, almost half (82) are collections of poems and essays (I owe this latter reference to Kang-i Sun Chang).

NOTES

48. Yeh Ting-yi ("T'ang Wu-tai Tz'u Lüeh-shu," p. 116) suggests that the lyrics of Li Hsün, one of the *Hua-chien* poets, were the first to be edited as a separate collection by a single poet. If this was done by Li himself, it was an early exception. For a discussion of the *Tsun-ch'ien Chi*, see my "Textual Notes."

49. For poems recovered from Fang Hui's anthology, see Appendix A, poems XI–XII.

50. See Bryant, "Textual Notes," and "The Hsieh Hsin En Fragments," for a discussion of several poems by Li Yü that involve particularly trying textual dilemmas.

51. Yu Mou, *Sui-ch'u T'ang Shu-mu*, 50ab.

52. Ch'en Chen-sun, *Chih-chai Shu-lu Chieh-t'i*, 21.1b.

53. For Pai P'u's poem, see his *T'ien-lai Chi*, A.3b–4a (1273). For a discussion of the relationship between this poem and those of Li Yü, Chiang Li-tsai, *Li Hou-chu Tz'u-chuan*, p. 87.

Selections from the YANG-CH'UN CHI

I. To "Ch'üeh T'a Chih" (I)

muai	lak	vhan	tši	ts'ien	van-	p'yian-
yiu	dzhɨ-	tâ	dzhing			
xhyak	süat	zhüi	fung	trüan-		
dzhak	yia-	šêng	kâ	yüong	yi-	san-
tsiu:	sing	t'iam	têk	džhêu	vuê	xhyan-

lêu	žhiang-	tš'ün	šan	xhan	sɨ-	myian-
kuâ	dzhin-	tšing	xhong			
muê-	king:	.yien	šim	ts'ian:		
.yit	šiang:	bhing-	lan	rin	put	kyian-
kyau	siau	.iam:	lüi-	sɨ	liang	pyian-

Plum blossoms shed from lavish boughs, a thousand million petals:
As though with tender hearts themselves,
In snowflake fashion they tumble along with the wind.
Yesterday evening's pipes and singing were casually dismissed;
Awakening from wine only adds to sorrow without end.

From atop a pavilion, springtime hills stand cold on every side;
The geese on their journey have all gone by;
Haze thins and thickens in evening sunlight.
I lean for a moment against the railing, but no one can be seen;
Mermaid silk holds back the tears as I think it all through again.

Mermaid silk: a kind of thin pongee woven, according to Chinese legend, by woman-like creatures that lived beneath the waters of the South China Sea. "Mermaid" is only an approximation; the Chinese word, *chiao*, is cognate with a word for "shark."

II. To "Ch'üeh T'a Chih" (II)

žhüi	dhau-	xhyan	dzhing	p'au	drhik	kiu:
muai:	tau-	tš'ün	lai			
tr'iu	tr'iang-	xhwan	.i	ghiu-		
ghiu-	rit	xwa	dzhien	žhiang	bhing-	tsiu:
kam:	zhɨ	king-	li: ·	tšüê	ngyan	šêu-

xhâ	bhuan-	ts'ing	vuê	ti	žhiang-	liu:
üi-	vun-	sin	džhêu			
xhâ	žhɨ-	nien	nien	iu:		
dhok	lip	siau:	lêu	fung	muan:	zhiu-
bhing	lim	sin	ngüat	rin	küi	xhêu-

Who would have thought a carefree heart could be cast away for ever?
Every year when spring arrives,
Sorrow and remorse abide unchanged.
In bygone days beside the blossoms I was always drunk on wine;
Oh, to avoid the mirrors in which my rosy face grows thin!

Green weeds by river banks, willows on the dikes—
And yet I wonder at new sorrow;
On what account does it arise, year after year?
Standing alone on a tiny pavilion, the wind billowing my sleeves,
And a new moon above the wooded plain after everyone has gone
    home....

III. To "Ch'üeh T'a Chih" (III)

ts'iu	rip	muan	tsiau	fung	puan-	liat
lang	dzhik	drhi	dhang			
üê:	têng:	šê	xhâ	tšiat		
riau:	ts'i-	ghüong	šing	fang	ts'au:	xiat
džhêu	drhiang	xhyak	dzhin-	ting	xiang	kyiat
xhuai	šiu:	si	nam	k'an	van:	ngüat
kuê	ngyan-	lai	žhi			
sai-	kuan:	šing	ming	.yiat		
lik	lik	dzhien	xuan	vuê	tš'iê-	yüat
kwan	šan	xhâ	rit	xiu	li	bhiat

Autumn has come to the banana leaves, blown now half to shreds;
Tattered and torn, the ponds and pools,
Where rain beats down and breaks off scattered lotus.
Around the steps the cries of crickets die away in fragrant grass;
My aching heart is knotted as hard as a new wisteria bud.

I turn back toward the southwest and look at the evening moon;
A solitary goose comes flying over:
Moaning and sobbing, the sound of frontier flutes.
One after another, the old pleasures, nowhere to be enjoyed;
When will these towering mountains cease to keep us far apart?

IV. To "Ch'üeh T'a Chih" (IV)

xwa	nguai-	xhan	kyi	t'ien	yüok	žhiê-
xiang	.yin-	žhing	xuai			
k'i:	dzhuâ-	xhun	vuê	zhiê-		
yiam	tsi-	kau	dhong	nging	siok	vuê-
küan:	liam	šwang	ts'iak	king	fyi	k'iê-

bhying	žhiang-	lâ	.i	xhyan	siu-	lüê:
.yit	šiang:	kwan	dzhing			
.ik	pyian-	kyang	nam	luê-		
yia-	yia-	mong-	xhun	xiu	muan-	ngiê:
yi:	tri	dzhien	žhɨ-	vuê	zhim	tš'iê-

Beyond the blossoms, cold cockcrow, the day about to dawn:
Incense cakes have turned to ashes;
Up or at rest, I am utterly distracted.
Tall phoenix trees at the edge of the eaves transfix the overnight fog;
I roll up the blinds and a pair of magpies flies away in alarm.

Draped over a screen, a gossamer gown, idle embroidered strands;
Just for a moment my heart is full,
As I remember all the roads of the sunny south.
Night after night my dreaming soul gives up its empty fantasies,
For now I know that nowhere can the bygone past be sought.

V. To "Ch'üeh T'a Chih" (V)

p'uâ:	nai-	üi	rin	dzhing	t'ai-	bhak
ki:	dhuê-	sɨ	liang			
tšin	ngi:	xhun	p'au	k'iak		
sin	kyiat	dhong	sim	xiang	vyi-	lak
tsim:	**šêng**	vhu-	têk	tang	tš'ê	.iak

xiu	xiang-	tsun	dzhien	dzhing	sak	mak
šiu:	kiê:	kim	luai			
bhing	drhiang-	**šim**	šim	tšiak		
mak	sin-	têng:	xhyan	siang	têu-	tsak
yiê:	kün	puau:	ts'üê:	drhiang	xuan	lak

How hateful it is that men should have such shallow hearts;
Many times I have thought it through,
And truly would rather cast it all aside!
When the knot of love is newly tied, its fragrance still not faded,
One ought to honour, no matter what, the bond already formed.

Do not feel so weary at heart with wine before you there;
But hold aloft a golden flagon
And just for me drink deep and full.
Let's not waste our time on pointless banter back and forth;
I promise to share my joy and happiness with you forever!

VI. To "Ch'üeh T'a Chih" (VI)

siau	sak	ts'ing	ts'iu	tšüê	lüi-	drhüi-
tšim:	dhiam-	vyi	liang			
trian:	trüan-	xhun	vuê	myi-		
dzhan	tsiu:	yüok	sing	triong	yia-	k'i:
ngüat	ming	riê	lian-	t'ien	riê	šüi:
kyai	xhya-	xhan	šing	dhi	lak	üi-
dhing	žhüê-	kim	fung			
ts'iau:	ts'iau:	drhüong	mun	pyi-		
k'â:	sik	ghiu-	xuan	xhyüi	šiu:	dhi-
sɨ	liang	.yit	zhik	žhing	dzhiau	dzhüi-

Mournful and forlorn in clear autumn, tears drop like pearls;
Pillow and mat are faintly cool,
As I toss and turn, unable to sleep at all.
Almost sober, wine wearing off, I get up in the dead of night:
The moon as bright as glossed silk, the heavens as a river.

Below the steps, the cold chatter of chirping weaver-crickets;
An autumnal breeze in the garden trees,
Quiet and still, behind double barred gates.
How sad I feel for bygone joys, the places we went hand in hand;
Thinking this over all night long, I grow weary and haggard at last.

VII. To "Ch'üeh T'a Chih" (VII)

vhan	nau:	žhiau	kuang	nêng	ki:	xiê:
drhiang	dhuan-	xhun	siau			
k'an	k'iak	tš'ün	xhwan	k'iê-		
tši	xi:	dzhiang	dhêu	ling	ts'iak	ngiê:
put	tri	ts'ing	tiau:	dzhüen	siang	nguê-

sim	riak	žhüi	yiang	ts'ien	van-	lüê:
šüi:	k'uat	xwa	fyi			
mong-	dhuan-	vuê	šan	luê-		
k'ai	ngyan:	sin	džhêu	vuê	vun-	tš'iê-
tšüê	liam	kim:	triang-	siang	si	fu:

This vernal radiance that torments my thoughts, how much longer
    will it abide?
My heart is broken and my spirit overcome,
To see that spring has withdrawn once again.
I rejoiced in the tale of an elfin magpie perched upon the wall,
Little knowing the goddess's blackbirds would utterly betray me.

My heart is like the thousand million strands that trail from the willows.
The river is broad, the blossoms fly;
My dream is broken on the road to Shamanka Hill.
I open my eyes to new sorrow, whose source cannot be found;
Beaded blinds and brocade curtains—was it love or was it not?

Blackbirds: See the *Han-Wu Ku-shih* attributed to Pan Ku, "On the seventh day of the seventh
month, while the Emperor was at the Ch'eng-hua Palace, there suddenly appeared, just at noon
of the fast day, a black bird, which flew in from the West and came to roost before the Palace.
The Emperor asked Tung-fang Shuo about it, and Shuo replied, 'This means that the Queen
Mother of the West is about to arrive.' After a moment, the Queen Mother did arrive, with two
birds, black like ravens, in attendance, one on either side" (quoted from the *T'ai-p'ing Yü-lan*,
927.3a [4252], with textual corrections from the fuller version of the story in Ch'ao Tsai-chih's
Hsü T'an-chu, 3.29b–30b).

VIII. To "Ch'üeh T'a Chih" (VIII)

šwang	lak	siau:	üen	yiau	ts'au:	tuan:
šêu-	yiap	xhuâ	fung			
tr'iu	tr'iang-	fang	žhi	xhuan-		
ghiu-	xhên-	nien	nien	ts'iu	put	kuan:
mong	long	riê	mong-	k'ong	drhiang	dhuan-

dhok	lip	xuang	drhi	zhia	rit	ngan-
dzhiang	nguai-	yiau	šan			
.in:	.in:	lien	t'ien	xan-		
xut	.ik	tang	nien	kâ	vuê:	bhuan-
van:	lai	šwang	lam:	dhi	xhên	muan:

Frost forms in a tiny garden where nephrite grass is short;
Thin leaves rustle in the wind,
Mournful and forlorn, their fragrant season expires.
Ancient heart-ache comes year after year, but autumn is indifferent;
Vague, uncertain, as in a dream—my heart broken for nothing.

I stand alone in slanting sunlight on the bank of a weed-filled pond;
Beyond the wall are distant hills
Leading dim and dark to the Heavenly River.
A fleeting memory of my partner in song and dancing years ago,
And all evening long my cheeks are flooded by traces of my sobs....

IX. To "Ch'üeh T'a Chih" (IX)

fang	ts'au:	muan:	üen	xwa	muan:	mok
liam	nguai-	vyi	vyi			
si-	üê:	long	dhing	triok		
yiang	liu:	ts'ien	dhiau	tšüê	lok	sok
pik	drhi	puâ	tšêu-	.üen	.iang	yüok
.yiau:	dhiau:	rin	kya	ngyan	riê-	ngüok
xhyien	kuan:	ling	ling			
dzhi	tsêu-	ün	xhuâ	k'üok		
kong	tsɨ:	xuan	yien	yiu	vyi-	tsüok
zhia	yiang	put	yüong-	siang	ts'uai	ts'üok

Fragrant verdure fills the courtyard; blossoms fill our eyes;
Fragile and soft outside the blinds,
A fine rain enshrouds the garden bamboo.
Weeping willows trail a thousand strands of beaded leaves;
Ripples veil a jade pool where bridal ducks are bathing.

Shy and demure, a certain someone with features just like jade:
Strings and flutes sound clear and pure,
Performing in unison the Song of Cloud-like Harmony.
A youthful lord is enjoying the banquet, but still he feels a lack;
No point in having the slanting sunlight try to hurry him on.

Song of Cloud-like Harmony: a piece of court music believed to be of great antiquity.

X. To "Ch'üeh T'a Chih" (X)

ki:	dhuê-	vhung-	lêu	dhong	.im:	.yian-
ts'ɨ:	zhik	siang	vhung			
k'iak	šing-	tang	žhi	kyian-		
ti	ngiê-	dzhien	xuan	bhyin	trüan:	myian-
šwang	mi	liam:	xhên-	tš'ün	šan	üan:

lap	tšüok	lüi-	liu	k'iang	dhik	.üan-
t'êu	tšing:	lâ	.i			
yüok	tš'iang-	dzhing	yiu	lan:		
tsüi-	li:	put	zhɨ	kim	tšan:	muan:
yiang	kwan	.yit	k'üok	drhiang	ts'ien	dhuan-

So many times we drank and feasted together in the Phoenix Pavilion;
But now this evening we meet again,
And it means much more than it did in times gone by.
Speaking softly of former joys, averting our faces time and again:
Heart-ache gathered in a pair of brows—springtime hills so far away....

Teardrops flow from wax candles as nomad flutes complain;
Furtively straightening her gossamer gown,
About to sing, but still at heart reluctant....
Once drunk she cannot refuse a brimming golden bowl;
The *Yang-kuan* farewell song alone will break her heart a thousand
times.

The *Yang-kuan* song: Yang-kuan Pass was the last frontier point as one left China on the way
into Central Asia. The farewell song was actually this poem by Wang Wei, written for a friend
who was leaving on a trip to the far West:

On Saying Farewell to Yuan Erh, Who is Leaving on a Mission to An-hsi

At Wei-ch'eng a morning rain has dampened the fine dust;
By a travellers' inn, the fresh charm of green green willows....
I urge you now to finish off a single cup of wine;
Once you are west of Yang-kuan Pass you will find no friends.

(*Wang Yu-ch'eng Chi Chien-chu*, 14.363)

XI. To "Ch'üeh T'a Chih" (XI)

ki:	rit	xhying	ün	xhâ	tš'iê-	k'iê-
vang-	k'iak	küi	lai			
put	dhau-	tš'ün	tsiang	muê-		
pêk	ts'au:	ts'ien	xwa	xhan	žhik	luê-
xiang	kiê	kyi-	dzhai-	žhüi	kya	žhüê-

lüi-	ngyan:	.i:	lêu	bhyin	dhok	ngiê-
šwang	.yian-	fyi	lai			
mêk	žhiang-	siang	vhung	fu:		
liau:	luan-	tš'ün	džhêu	riê	liu:	siê-
yiu	yiu	mong-	li:	vuê	zhim	tš'iê-

For how many days do the clouds drive on, where do they finally go?
They have forgotten to come home,
Little knowing that spring is almost over.
A hundred herbs, a thousand blossoms, by the roads at Cold Food time;
Before whose house the tree to which your fragrant carriage is tethered?

With tear-filled eyes beside a pavilion, she murmurs to herself;
A pair of swallows comes flying by:
"Did you meet him along the path?"
This pervasive troubling springtime sorrow is like the willow catkins,
Far and wide, within a dream that nowhere can be sought.

XII. To "Ch'üeh T'a Chih" (XII)

```
dhing    üan-      šim      šim       šim      ki:      xiê:
yiang    liu:      tuai     .yien
liam     mak       vuê      drhüong   šuê-
ngüok    lêk       tiau     .an       yiu      yia:     tš'iê-
lêu      kau       put      kyian-    tšiang   dhai     luê-

üê:      xhwêng-   fung     ghüang    sam      ngüat    muê-
mun      .iam:     xhuang   xun
vuê      kyi-      liu      tš'ün     drhüê-
lüi-     ngyan:    vun-     xwa       xwa      put      ngiê-
luan-    xhong     fyi      rip       ts'iu    ts'ien   k'iê-
```

Courtyard and garden deep and remote, how deep and remote indeed?
Weeping willows, banks of mist,
Blinds and curtains in layers beyond count.
Jade bridle and inlaid saddle gone to the pleasure grounds,
The pavilion is tall, but the road to Resplendent Terrace cannot be seen.

The rain is wayward, the wind erratic, as the Third Month draws to
     a close;
A doorway barred on yellow twilight—
No device will make this spring abide.
Eyes filled with teardrops question the blossoms; the blossoms do not
     reply:
A flurry of scarlet flies away into the hanging swings.

XIII. To "Ch'üeh T'a Chih" (XIII)

fun:	.ing-	dzhiang	dhêu	xhan	yüok	dzhin-
kiong	lêu-	drhiang	žhi			
tsiu:	sing:	rin	yiu	k'un-		
.yit	tiam:	tš'ün	sim	vuê	xhyan-	xhên-
lâ	.i	.yin-	muan:	dhi	tšwang	fun:

liu:	ngan-	xwa	fyi	xhan	žhik	ghin-
mêk	žhiang-	xhying	rin			
.yiau:	put	drhüen	fang	sin-		
lêu	žhiang-	drhüong	yiam	šan	.in:	.in:
tong	fung	dzhin-	rit	tš'üi	žhien	pyin-

Glaring white, a white-washed wall, cold weather almost over;
Long hours pass on a palace clock;
Someone suffers still, as the wine wears off.
A single dab of spring emotion, heart-ache without end,
A gossamer gown is printed all over with "teardrop traces" powder.

Blossoms fly from willow banks as Cold Food time approaches;
The people walking along the paths
Never bring her fragrant letters from far away.
Atop a pavilion, layered eaves, mountains dim and dark....
An east wind, all day long, blows her cicada hairdress.

XIV. To "Ch'üeh T'a Chih" (XIV)

liok	k'üok	lan	kan	.uai	pik	žhüê-
yiang	liu:	fung	k'ying			
trian:	dzhin-	xhuang	kim	lüê:		
žhüi	pa:	dhien	tšêng	yi	ngüok	drhüê-
tš'üen	liam	xai:	.yian-	king	fyi	k'iê-

muan:	ngyan:	yiu	sɨ	kyiam	lak	siê-
xhong	xhying-	k'ai	žhi			
.yit	šap	ts'ing	ming	üê:		
nrüong	žhüi-	kyak	lai	.ying	luan-	ngiê:
king	dzhan	xau:	mong-	vuê	zhim	tš'iê-

In sixfold meanders the balustrade caresses jade-green trees;
The weeping willows in a gentle breeze
Bring forth all their golden yellow strands.
Someone takes up an inlaid lute and adjusts its pegs of jade;
Breaching the blinds, a startled swallow flies away in alarm.

As far as eyes can see, floating gossamer and drifting catkins;
Scarlet apricot blossoms unfold
In a brief spell of Ch'ing-ming season rain.
Just aroused from heavy slumber to the random chatter of orioles,
Startled from the ruins of a happy dream that nowhere can be sought....

XV. To "Ts'ai Sang-tzu" (I)

siau:	dhing	üê:	kuâ-	tš'ün	tsiang	dzhin-
p'yian-	p'yian-	xwa	fyi			
dhok	tšiat	dzhan	tši			
vuê	ngiê:	bhing	lan	tši	dzhɨ-	tri

ngüok	dhang	xiang	nuan:	tšüê	liam	küan:
šwang	.yian-	lai	küi			
ghiu-	.iak	nan	ghi			
k'êng:	sin-	žhiau	xhwa	têk	ki:	žhi

In a tiny garden the rain is over, and spring is almost gone;
Petal by petal the blossoms fly;
Alone I break off a tattered spray
And lean against a railing, silent, communing with myself.

Incense is warm in the jade hall as beaded blinds are raised;
A pair of swallows coming home....
Old promises are hard to keep:
How well I know the bloom of youth lasts but a little while.

XVI. To "Ts'ai Sang-tzu" (II)

ma:	si	rin	ngiê:	tš'ün	fung	ngan-
fang	ts'au:	myien	myien			
yiang	liu:	ghiau	pyien			
lak	rit	kau	lêu	tsiu:	bhuai-	xhyüen

ghiu-	džhêu	sin	xhên-	tri	tâ	šiau:
mok	dhuan-	yiau	t'ien			
dhok	lip	xwa	dzhien			
kyêng-	t'ing-	šêng	kâ	muan:	xhwa-	žhüen

A horse's neigh and the sound of voices on a shore where the spring
   breeze blows;
Fragrant herbs stretch on and on,
There are weeping willows beside the bridge,
And a wineshop banner hanging from a tall pavilion in the setting sun.

Who can reckon the sum of old sorrow and new heart-ache?
The distant heavens lost to sight....
I stand alone beside the blossoms,
And hear pipes and singing fill the painted barges once again.

XVII. To "Ts'ai Sang-tzu" (III)

si	fung	puan-	yia-	liam	long	lêng:
üan:	mong-	tš'ê	küi			
...	kuâ-	kim	fyi			
xwa	zhia-	tš'wang	dzhien	yia-	xhap	tši

tšiau	yiang	dhian-	li:	sin	fan	k'üok
vyi-	iu:	rin	tri			
t'êu	ts'üê:	šêng	tš'üi			
king	kyak	xhan	ghüong	tau-	xyiau:	dhi

A wind from the west in the dead of night—latticed blinds are cold;
Just returned from a far away dream,
(...) past golden doors,
As blossoms drop from the boughs of mimosa trees outside the window.

Within the halls of Chao-yang Palace, a song newly arranged,
That no one at all has ever heard.
She takes up her pipes and blows a furtive note,
Waking with a start the chill crickets that cry all through the night.

XVIII. To "Ts'ai Sang-tzu" (IV)

tsiu:	lan	žhüi-	kyak	t'ien	xiang	nuan:
siu-	xhuê-	žhüong	k'ai			
xiang	.yin-	žhing	xuai			
dhok	bhuai-	xhan	bhying	li:	ghiu-	mi
mong	long	k'iak	xiang-	têng	dzhien	nguâ-
tš'wang	ngüat	bhuai	xhuai			
xyiau:	mong-	tš'ê	xhuai			
.yit	yia-	tong	fung	drhan-	tsau:	muai

The banquet over, aroused from sleep to the warmth of heavenly incense:
Brocaded doors left heedlessly ajar,
Incense cakes reduced to ashes,
Alone, she turns away from a cold screen to redo her faded brows.

Dim and hazy there where she lies back down beside the lamp,
The moon in the window lingers a while.
Just returned from a daybreak dream:
A single evening of easterly wind has burst the blossoming plums.

XIX. To "Ts'ai Sang-tzu" (V)

siau:	dhang	šim	dzhing-	vuê	rin	tau-
muan:	üan-	tš'ün	fung			
tr'iu	tr'iang-	dzhiang	tong			
.yit	žhüê-	.ying	dhau	tai-	üê:	xhong

džhêu	sim	zhɨ-	tsüi-	kyiam	riê	bhing-
yüok	ngiê-	xhwan	žhüong			
rit	muê-	šê	tšüong			
šwang	.yian-	küi	si	xhwa-	kak	triong

By a tiny house, secluded and quiet, where no one ever comes,
Filling the courtyard, a spring breeze—
Mournful and forlorn east of the wall,
A cherry tree covered with blossoms, pink and touched with raindrops.

A sorrowing heart seems as though drunk, or even ill,
About to speak, but still reluctant....
As the sun fades, scattered bells,
And a pair of swallows flying home to roost in a painted hall.

XX. To "Ts'ai Sang-tzu" (VI)

xhwa-	dhang	têng	nuan:	liam	long	küan:
kim-	lêu-	trêng	trêng			
üê:	bha-	xhan	šêng			
.yit	yia-	si	tš'wang	mong-	put	žhing

ngüok	ngâ	drhüong-	k'i:	t'iam	xiang	.yin-
xhuai	.i:	kuê	bhying			
put	ngiê-	xham	dzhing			
šüi:	dhiau-	xhâ	rin	tš'üi	dhik	šing

In a painted hall the lamps are warm, latticed blinds rolled up;
Palace clocks run stroke by stroke;
As rain dies away the cold is born;
All night long, in her western window, a dream she cannot finish.

A lady of jade gets up again to add an incense cake,
Returns to lean on a single screen,
Saying nothing, holding back....
The sound of someone playing the "River Song" on a bamboo flute—

"River Song": a piece of music popular during the T'ang dynasty.

XXI. To "Ts'ai Sang-tzu" (VII)

šêng	kâ	fang-	san-	rin	küi	k'iê-
dhok	siok	kyang	lêu			
ngüat	žhiang:	ün	šiu			
.yit	puan-	tšüê	liam	kwa-	ngüok	kêu

k'i:	lai	tiam:	kiam:	kying	yiu	dhi-
tš'iê-	tš'iê-	sin	džhêu			
bhing	drhiang-	tong	liu			
tsiang	ts'üê:	li	sim	kuâ	kyüt	tšiu

Pipes and singers dismissed and scattered, everyone gone home;
I spend the night alone in a pavilion by the river.
The moon rises, clouds withdraw....
Half the beaded blinds are hanging up on their hooks of jade.

I get up and take stock again of the lands where I have been;
There is sorrow anew in place after place.
I would trouble the eastward flowing stream
To carry this stranger heart of mine away to Orange Isle.

Orange Isle: a man named Li Heng (third century) planted a thousand orange trees back in his native district so that his family would have a resource to fall back on in times of trouble. See Hsi Tso-ch'ih, *Hsiang-yang ch'i-chiu chi*, 2.9b.

XXII. To "Ts'ai Sang-tzu" (VIII)

tšiau	yiang	ki-	têk	žhin	sien	liê:
dhok	dzhï-	žhing	.ên			
šüi:	dhian-	têng	xun			
lâ	mak	k'ying	xhan	yia-	tšing-	tš'ün

riê	kim	bhiat	kuan-	t'iam	siau	sak
muan:	myian-	dhi	xhên			
ghiu-	.iak	yiu	dzhun			
rin:	pa:	kim	xhwan	bhiat	yiê:	rin

In Chao-yang Palace is called to mind a companion of gods and spirits,
Who enjoyed favour all to herself.
A river mansion in lamplit twilight,
Gossamer curtains in the slight chill of an evening at the height of
    spring....

But now instead in separate quarters, ever more desolate and dreary,
Her whole face streaked with weeping:
"If our former bond were still to be kept,
How could you bear to give my golden ring to someone else?"

XXIII. To "Ts'ai Sang-tzu" (IX)

vyi	fung	liam	mak	ts'ing	ming	ghin-
xwa	lak	tš'ün	dzhan			
tsun	tsiu:	liu	xuan			
t'iam	dzhin-	lâ	.i	k'iap	yia-	xhan

džhêu	ngyan	k'yap	zhɨ-	šiau	dzhan	tšüok
tšüê	lüi-	lan	kan			
yia:	yüok	kau	p'uan			
tšêng	nai-	siang	vhung	dzhing	van-	puan

A faint breeze stirs blinds and curtains as Ch'ing-ming time draws near;
Blossoms fall and spring fades away.
A cup of wine to keep me happy,
Even with all my gossamer garments I fear the chill of evening.

A sorrowing face is just like a candle burnt away to nothing,
Pearl-like teardrops here and there.
I wish I could leave this all behind,
For how could I bear to meet you and feel a million different longings
   in my heart?

XXIV. To "Ts'ai Sang-tzu" (X)

xhwa-	dhang	dzhak	yia-	džhêu	vuê	žhüi-
fung	üê:	ts'i	ts'i			
lim	ts'iak	tan	si			
lak	dzhin-	têng	xwa	kyi	vyi-	dhi

nien	kuang	üang:	žhɨ-	riê	liu	šüi:
xiu	šüat	dzhing	myi			
ngüok	drhiê-	šwang	žhüi			
tši	žhi-	kim	long	.ying	vuê:	tri

In a painted hall last night I could not sleep for sorrow,
Wind and rain so cold and drear;
Magpies were roosting alone in the grove,
Lamplight blossoms faded and vanished, but cockcrow did not come.

The beauty of the year and bygone days are like a flowing river;
Do not speak of love's enchantments.
Jade streams flow down my cheeks,
And only the parrot closed in its golden cage can know the cause.

XXV. To "Ts'ai Sang-tzu" (XI)

xhan	žhien	yüok	puau-	sam	ts'iu	xhêu-
dzhik	dzhing-	.yiu	tšai			
yiap	lak	xhyan	kyai			
ngüat	t'êu-	liam	long	üan:	mong-	xhuai

tšiau	yiang	ghiu-	xhên-	.i	dzhien	dzhai-
xiu	šüat	tang	žhi			
ngüok	dhik	dzhai	tš'üi			
muan:	zhiu-	šêng	šêng	xyüat	iu-	žhüi

A chill cicada has come to announce the season, end of autumn;
By a secluded chamber, still and remote,
Leaves are shed on idle steps;
Moonlight filters through latticed blinds on return from a faraway
  dream.

The ancient heart-ache of Chao-yang Palace remains the same as ever;
Do not speak of times gone by.
A jade flute has just begun to sound,
But full sleeves, red as monkey's blood, still hang limp.

XXVI. To "Ts'ai Sang-tzu" (XII)

dhong-	vhang	šim	yia-	šêng	kâ	san-
liam	mak	drhüong	drhüong			
zhia	ngüat	mong	long			
üê:	kuâ-	dzhan	xwa	lak	dhi-	xhong

sik	nien	vuê	xhyan-	šiang	sim	žhi-
.i	ghiu-	tong	fung			
dhok	.i:	nguê	dhong			
xhyan	siang:	xhyan	sɨ	tau-	xyiau:	tšüong

In a secluded boudoir in the depth of night, pipes and song dismissed:
Blinds and curtains in layer after layer,
Slanting moonlight hazy and dim;
The rains are over—tattered blossoms fallen scarlet upon the ground . . . .

No end of things from bygone years that are a source of heart-ache;
The east wind abides unchanged—
Leaning alone by a phoenix tree,
In idle thoughts and idle longing until the bells of dawn.

XXVII. To "Ts'ai Sang-tzu" (XIII)

xwa   dzhien   šit   k'iak   yiu   tš'ün   liê:
dhok   dzhɨ-   zhim   fang
muan: mok   pi   liang
tsüong- iu: šêng   kâ   yik   dhuan-   drhiang

lim   kyan   xi-   dhiap   liam   kyan   .yian-
kak   dzhɨ-   šwang   šwang
rin: kyêng-   sɨ   liang
lüok   žhüê-   ts'ing   dhai   puan- zhik   yiang

Beside the blossoms I have lost my companion in springtime roaming;
Alone I go in search of fragrance;
Grief and sorrow as far as eyes can see;
Even were there pipes and singing, my heart would still be broken.

Within the grove are sporting butterflies, swallows among the blinds;
Each with each they go in pairs;
I cannot bear to weight and ponder:
Green trees and dark moss divide the evening sunlight....

XXVIII. To "Chiu Ch'üan-tzu" (IV)

```
fang    ts'au:  drhiang  tš'üen
liu:    .ing-   ngüi     ghiau   ghiau  xhya-   luê-
küi     xhong   fyi
xhying  rin     k'iê-
pik     šan     pyien

fung    vyi     .yien    dham-   üê:    siau    rien
kyêk    ngan-   ma:      si      xhâ    tš'iê-
kiu:    xhuai   drhiang
šwang   lam:    lüi-
zhik    yiang   t'ien
```

Fragrant herbs and a long river,
Willows outline a high-arched bridge and a path beneath the bridge.
Geese are flying homeward,
My wanderer has gone,
Beyond the emerald hills.

The breeze is faint, the mist pale, the rain chill and drear;
On the far shore a horse neighs, somewhere....
Heart tied in knots,
Tear-stained cheeks,
The sky in evening sunlight....

XXIX. To "Lin Chiang Hsien" (II)

lêng:	xhong	p'yiau	k'i:	dhau	xwa	p'yian-
ts'ing	tš'ün	.i-	zhiê-	lan	san	
xhwa-	lêu	liam	mak	küan:	k'ying	xhan
tsiu:	yiê	rin	san-	xhêu-		
dhok	dzhi-	bhing	lan	kan		

zhik	yiang	ts'ien	li:	lien	fang	ts'au:
ts'i	ts'i	džhêu	šai-	üang	sun	
bhuai	xhuai	fyi	dzhin-	pik	t'ien	ün
vhung-	šêng	xhâ	tš'iê-			
ming	ngüat	tšiau-	xhuang	xun		

Cold scarlet floats aloft, peach blossom petals,
Strands of springtime mood in weary disarray....
In a slight chill, with the curtains and blinds of a painted pavilion rolled,
After the banquet, once everyone has gone,
All alone, she leans against a balustrade.

Fragrant herbs extend a thousand leagues in evening sunlight;
So lush and green—pangs of sorrow for a wandering prince.
To and fro, flown all away, the clouds in a jade-blue sky;
Somewhere the sound of phoenix pipes,
And a radiant moon aglow on yellow twilight.

XXX. To "Ch'ing-p'ing Yüeh" (II)

üê:	dzhing	.yien	van:			
lüok	šüi:	sin	drhi	muan:		
šwang	.yian-	fyi	lai	žhüi	liu:	üan-
siau:	kak	xhwa-	liam	kau	küan:	

xhuang	xun	dhok	.i:	tšüê	lan
si	nam	sin	ngüat	mi	.wan
ts'i-	xhya-	lak	xwa	fung	k'i:
lâ	.i	dhêk	dhi-	tš'ün	xhan

A misty evening as rain clears up
And green water swells in new pools;
A pair of swallows flies into a courtyard where willows trail;
The painted blinds of a tiny pavilion are rolled up high.

Leaning alone on a vermilion balustrade in yellow twilight,
The arched eyebrow of a new moon to the southwest....
Fallen blossoms below the steps are stirred by a breeze,
And the chill of spring is felt most of all through a gossamer gown....

XXXI. To "Tsui Hua Chien" (III)

```
dzhing   süat    siau:   üen     tš'ün   vyi-    tau-
drhi     pyien   muai    dzhi-   tsau:
kau      žhüê-   ts'iak  xhyam   džhau-
zhia     ngüat   ming    xhan    ts'au:

šan      tš'üen  fung    king:   xau:
dzhi-    kuê:    kim     ling    dhau-
šiau-    nien    k'an    k'iak   lau:
siang    vhung   mak     .yiam-  tsüi-   kim     puai
bhiat    li      tâ
xuan     xhuai-  šiau:
```

It clears after snow in a tiny garden that spring has not yet reached;
Along the pond the plums blossom early of themselves.
Magpies carry their nesting to lofty trees,
And slanting moonlight illumines wintry weeds.

Beautiful, this view of hills and streams,
As always along the roads of Chin-ling town;
But youth turns to age all the same....
Weary not, when we meet, of getting drunk from golden cups;
Of partings there are many,
Of happy meetings, few.

XXXII. To "Yeh Chin Men" (II)

yiang	liu:	mêk			
puau:	ma:	si	k'ong	vuê	tsik
sin	triak	xhâ	.i	rin	vyi-	šik
nien	nien	kyang	xai:	k'yêk	

mong-	kyak	vuê	šan	tš'ün	šêk
tsüi-	ngyan:	xwa	fyi	lang	dzhik
k'i:	vuê:	put	zhɨ	vuê	k'i-	lik
.ai-	kün	tš'üi	ngüok	dhik	

A path lined with willows—
A fine horse neighs in the air—without a trace;
Newly dressed in a lotus gown, but recognized by no one,
Year after year a sojourner on lakes and streams....

Awakening from a dream of spring beauty on Shamanka Hill,
In drunken eyes the blossoms fly till all are gone.
Do not refuse to get up and dance, pleading you lack the strength—
Your sweetheart is playing the jade flute.

XXXIII. To "Yeh Chin Men" (IV)

fung	džha-	k'i:				
tš'üi	tšêu-	.yit	drhi	tš'ün	šüi:	
xhyan	yin:	.üen	.iang	xiang	kying-	li:
šiu:	suai	xhong	xhying-	rüi:		

têu-	.yap	lan	kan	dhok	.i:	
pik	ngüok	sau	dhêu	zhia	drhüi-	
tšiong	rit	vang-	kün	kün	put	tši-
kiê:	dhêu	vun	ts'iak	xi:		

A breeze about to rise
Blows ripples over a pool of spring water.
Idly leading bridal ducks along the fragrant paths,
Her hands push pink apricot blossoms aside.

She leans alone against the railing of a duck-fighting ring,
Green jade hairpins slipping loose....
"I have waited for you all day long; you have not come,
And looking up I hear the magpies' joy."

XXXIV. To "Kuei-tzu Yao" (I)

xhâ	tš'iê-	dhik				
tšiong	yia-	mong-	xhun	dzhing	mêk	mêk
triok	fung	yiam	üê:	xhan	tš'wang	tik

li	rin	šuê-	süi-	vuê	siau	sik
kim	dhêu	bhêk				
put	myien	dhêk	dhi-	drhüong	siang	.ik

Somewhere, a flute—
All night long a dreaming soul that trembles with silent longing;
A breeze in the bamboo, rain from the eaves, dripping in a cold window.

No word has come now for many years from one gone far away;
White-headed now,
Unable to sleep, she remembers him all the more.

XXXV. To "Kuei-tzu Yao" (II)

tš'ün	yiam-	yiam-				
kyang	žhiang-	van:	šan	sam	si-	tiam:
liu:	si	riê	tsian:	xwa	riê	riam:

xiang	kyüi	dzhik	dzhik	mun	puan-	.iam:
džhêu	mi	liam:				
lüi-	tšüê	tik	p'uâ-	.yien	tši	lam:

Spring glistens and glimmers:
Evening hills above the river, three or four dabs;
Willow catkins seem to be trimmed, blossoms to be dyed.

The scented boudoir is still and deserted, the doors are half-way shut;
Sorrowing brows contract,
And tear pearls drop and spatter on pink rouged cheeks.

XXXVI. To "Kuei-tzu Yao" (III)

xhan	šan	pik				
kyang	žhiang-	xhâ	rin	tš'üi	ngüok	dhik
p'yien	tšiu	üan:	song-	siau	siang	k'yêk

luê	xwa	ts'ien	li:	šwang	ngüat	bhêk
šiang	xhying	šêk				
lai	triau	bhyian-	žhi-	kwan	šan	kyêk

Cold hills jade green:
Out on the river, someone is playing a song on a flute of jade,
Saying farewell on a tiny boat, bound for the distant Hsiao and
    Hsiang....

A thousand leagues of flowering rushes, white in frosty moonlight;
Hurt by the look of departure—
By tomorrow already gone beyond these towering mountains.

The Hsiao and Hsiang: two rivers in southern Hunan, famed for their scenic beauty.

XXXVII. To "Nan Hsiang-tzu" (I)

```
si-     üê:     šip     liu     kuang
fang    ts'au:  nien    nien    yiê:    xhên-   drhiang
.yien   suâ:    vhung-  lêu     vuê     xhyan-  žhi-
mang    mang
luan    king-   .üen    kim     liang:  dhuan-  drhiang


xhun    mong-   rim     yiu     yiang
žhüi-   k'i:    yiang   xwa     muan:   siu-    džhwang
bhak    xhying- put     lai     mun     puan-   .iam:
zhia    yiang
vhu-    ni:     dzhan   tš'ün   lüi-    ki:     xhang
```

Fine rain dampens the glimmering light;
Fragrant herbs, year after year, grow along with my heart-ache.
Mist locks up the endless past of the Phoenix Pavilion,
Dim and dull;
The peacock mirror and bridal duck coverlets, alike they break one's
    heart.

A soul in dreams endures eternal drifting;
Asleep or awake, willow blossoms cover the embroidered bed.
A heartless lover hasn't come, the gate is half-way shut,
In slanting sunlight;
For you I bear a few streams of fading springtime tears....

XXXVIII. To "Ch'ang Ming Nü"

tš'ün	rit	.yian-				
lüok	tsiu:	.yit	puai	kâ	.yit	pyian-
tsai-	pai-	dhrin	sam	ngüan-		
.yit	ngüan-	lang	kün	ts'ien	süi-	
ri-	ngüan-	ts'iap	šin	žhiang	ghian-	
sam	ngüan-	riê	dhong	liang	žhiang-	.yian-
süi-	süi-	drhiang	siang	kyian-		

A banquet on a day in springtime:
A single cup of light wine, a single verse of song;
I bow twice and offer three wishes:
My first wish, that you, good sir, may live a thousand years;
My second, that your handmaid may keep her health forever;
My third, that like the swallows nesting in the rafters,
Year after year we may always be together.

XXXIX. To "Hsi Ch'ien Ying"

siok	.ying	dhi				
xiang	mong-	dhuan-				
tš'ün	žhüê-	xyiau:	mong	long		
dzhan	têng	xhuâ	zhin-	pyi-	tšüê	long
rin	ngiê:	kyêk	bhying	fung		

xiang	yi:	xhan				
têng	yi:	dzhüat				
xut	.ik	k'iê-	nien	li	bhiat	
žhik	žhing	xwa	üê:	.i:	kyang	lêu
puâ	žhiang-	mok	lan	tšiu		

Nesting warblers cry;
A dream of home is broken;
Spring trees are dim and hazy in the dawn.
The warm coals of fading lamps, closed in vermilion frames;
The sound of voices heard behind a screen....

Now the incense is cold;
Now the lamps are put out;
I suddenly remember our farewell last year.
In a rain of blossoms at Stone Wall Fort, by a pavilion along the River:
Your orchid boat afloat upon the waves....

Stone Wall: ancient fortifications guarding the approach to Nanking from upstream.

XL. To "Keng Lou-tzu" (V)

yia-   tš'ê   triang:
rin   ghin-   bhiat
mong-   dhuan- .yit   tš'wang dzhan   ngüat
.ying   vuê: žhüi-
xhyüi- kuê   ming
si   fung   xhan   vyi-   žhing

xhong   lap   tšüok
puan-   ghi   ghüok
džhwang žhiang- bhying fung   šan   lüok
kian: siu-   xhuang-
.i: yiau   ghim
dzhien xuan   lüi-   muan: kim

As nights begin to grow long,
And farewell draws near,
A dream is broken by the waning moon that fills the window.
The parrot is asleep;
A cicada is crying;
The west wind has not yet turned cold.

A red wax candle,
A chess match unfinished,
And hills green on a painted screen above the bed.
Lifting up an embroidered curtain,
Leaning over an inlaid lute,
Tears for bygone joys flood her gown....

XLI. To "P'ao Ch'iu Yüeh" (I)

tsiu:	bha-	kâ	yiê	xing-	vyi-	lan
siau:	ghiau	liu	šüi:	ghüong-	bhuan	xhuan
puâ	yiau	muai	rüi:	tang	sim	bhêk
fung	rip	lâ	.i	t'iap	t'i:	xhan
ts'ia:	mak	si	küi	k'iê-		
süê	dzhin-	šêng	kâ	ts'i:	zhik	xuan

The banquet over, singing done, excitement still unspent,
We linger a while by a tiny bridge across a flowing stream.
Stamens show white at the heart of plum blossoms bobbing on the
    ripples;
The wind blows through a gossamer gown pressed cold against my body.
But let us not think of going home just yet;
We must enjoy to the very end this night of pipes and song.

XLII. To "P'ao Ch'iu Yüeh" (II)

drhiok	šing-	küi	lai	üê:	vyi-	dzhing
lêu	dzhien	fung	drhüong-	ts'au:	.yien	k'ying
kok	.ying	ngiê:	rüan:	xwa	pyien	kuâ-
šüi:	dhiau-	šing	drhiang	tsüi-	li:	t'ing
k'uan:	kiê:	kim	kwêng	k'üan-		
žhüi	žhi-	tang	nien	tsuai-	iu:	dzhing

Since his return from repeated triumphs, the rain has not yet cleared:
The wind is strong outside the pavilion, mist is light on the grass.
Warblers in the glen murmur softly as they pass above the flowers;
Lingering notes of the "River Song" are heard in drunken ears.
Lazily raising a golden goblet, he demands,
"Who of all in bygone years possessed the most passionate heart!"

River Song: see above, poem XX.

XLIII. To "P'ao Ch'iu Yüeh" (III)

muai	lak	sin	tš'ün	rip	xhêu-	dhing
ngyan:	dzhien	fung	vut	k'â:	vuê	dzhing
k'üok	drhi	puâ	van:	ping	xhwan	xhap
fang	ts'au:	nging	žhüen	lüok	vyi-	žhing
ts'ia:	žhiang:	kau	lêu	vang-		
siang	ghüong-	bhing	lan	k'an	ngüat	šêng

Plum blossoms falling, early spring arrives in the inner gardens;
All that appears before our eyes, how lovely everything is!
Ripples come late to a meandering pool, the ice remaining firm;
Fragrant verdure welcomes our boats, though not yet fully green.
So let us climb a tall pavilion for the view;
Leaning together against a railing we shall watch as the moon is born.

XLIV. To "P'ao Ch'iu Yüeh" (IV)

nien	šiau-	üang	sun	iu:	tsün-	dzhai
têng	kau	xuan	tsüi-	yia-	vang	xhuai
kâ	lan	šiang:	dzhin-	san	xhuê	žhüê-
dzhing	xhêu-	drhüong	tšim	xuê:	p'êk	puai
dhan-	ngüan-	ts'ien	ts'ien	süi-		
kim	kiok	nien	nien	ts'iu	kyai:	k'ai

A wandering prince in the flower of youth, gifted with perfect genius,
Climbs the heights, joyously drunk, neglecting his home at night.
As singing fades, he admires in rapture the boughs of coral trees;
With hearty feeling, fills his amber flagon once again.
His only wish is a thousand thousand years
And golden chrysanthemums blooming in autumn, season after season.

XLV. To "P'ao Ch'iu Yüeh" (V)

šwang	tsik	ts'iu	šan	van-	žhüê-	xhong
.i:	ngyam	lêu	žhiang-	kwa-	tšüê	long
bhêk	ün	t'ien	üan:	drhüong	drhüong	xhên-
xhuang	ts'au:	.yien	šim	sik	sik	fung
fang:	fyi-	liang	tšiu	k'üok		
tš'üi	dzhai-	žhüi	kya	ngüok	dhik	triong

Frost collects on autumn hills—ten thousand trees turn red;
In a lofty pavilion close by a cliff is set a vermilion window.
White clouds distant in the sky, heart-ache in layer after layer;
Yellow grass deep in mist, a wind that moans and sighs.
That seems to be a Liang-chou Song
Played on a jade flute in someone's house....

Liang-chou Song: Liang-chou, in the west, gave its name to a kind of central Asian music very popular in the first half of the eighth century and well known afterward.

XLVI. To "P'ao Ch'iu Yüeh" (VI)

mak	.yiam-	têng	kau	bhêk	ngüok	puai
žhüê	yüê	vyi	drhan-	kiok	xwa	k'ai
drhi	dhang	šüi:	lêng:	.üen	.iang	k'i:
liam	mak	.yien	xhan	vhyi-	ts'üi-	lai
drhüong-	dhai-	šiau	xhong	tšüok		
liu	ts'üê:	šêng	kâ	mak	fang-	xhuai

Do not weary of climbing the heights with a white jade cup;
Dogwood leaves are barely opened, chrysanthemums in bloom.
The waters of ponds and pools turn cold—bridal ducks take flight;
In blinds and curtains the mist is wintry—kingfishers come flying.
And see that someone lights the scarlet candles,
Keep pipes and singing here with us; do not send them home.

XLVII. To "P'ao Ch'iu Yüeh" (VII)

dzhin-	rit	têng	kau	xing-	vyi-	dzhan
xhong	lêu	rin	san-	dhok	bhuan	xhuan
.yit	kêu	lêng:	vuê-	xhyüen	tšüê	bhak
muan:	myian-	si	fung	bhing	ngüok	lan
küi	k'iê-	süê	drhim	tsüi-		
siau:	üan-	sin	drhi	ngüat	džha-	xhan

Climbing the heights all day long, passion still unspent;
In a scarlet pavilion after all have gone, lingering on alone....
A single hook of cold fog suspends a beaded curtain;
Her face confronting the west wind, she leans on a jade balustrade.
Best to be really drunk when going home:
The moon newly cold on a fresh pool in the tiny courtyard....

XLVIII. To "P'ao Ch'iu Yüeh" (VIII)

dzhuâ-	tuai-	kau	lêu	ts'ien	van-	šan
ngyan-	fyi	ts'iu	šêk	muan:	lan	kan
šiau	dzhan	xhong	tšüok̥	muê-	ün	xhap
bhyiau	dzhin-	pik	nguê	kim	tsing:	xhan
tši:	tš'ik	rin	ts'ien	li:		
yiu	.ik	šêng	kâ	dzhak	yia-	xuan

Directly across from a lofty pavilion, a thousand million hills;
The beauty of autumn fills the balustrades as geese fly over.
Scarlet candles now burnt out, evening clouds converge;
By an emerald phoenix tree now blown bare, an autumnal well grown
  cold.
Just an inch, but for us a thousand leagues,
As still I remember the pipes and singing, last night's joy.

XLIX. To "Tsui T'ao-yuan" (I)

nam	üen	tš'ün	puan-	t'ap	ts'ing	žhi
fung	xhuâ	vun	ma:	si		
ts'ing	muai	riê	dhêu-	liu:	riê	mi
rit	drhiang	xhuê	dhiap	fyi		

xwa	luê-	drhüong-				
ts'au:	.yien	ti				
rin	kya	liam	mak	žhüi		
ts'iu	ts'ien	žhüong	k'un-	kyai:	lâ	.i
xhwa-	liang	šwang	.yian-	küi		

Spring half over in a southern garden, the season to "tread the green";
The breeze is mild, a horse's neigh is heard....
Green plums look like beans, willows look like eyebrows,
And all day long, the butterflies glide by.

Dew is heavy on the blossoms,
Mist low on the grass,
The blinds and curtains of people's houses hang.
Languid and lazy, sitting in a swing, she undoes her gossamer jacket
As a pair of swallows comes home to the painted bridge.

Tread the green: a festive occasion of early spring in central China.

L. To "Huan Hsi Sha" (IV)

trüan-	tšüok	p'yiau	bhong	.yit	mong-	küi
yüok	zhim	drhin	tsik	tr'iang-	rin	fyi
t'ien	kyau	sim	ngüan-	yiê:	šin	üi
dhai-	ngüat	drhi	dhai	k'ong	žhi-	šüi:
.im-	xwa	lêu	kak	muan-	zhia	xüi
têng	lim	put	sik	kyêng-	triam	.i

A candle's flicker, a floating wisp, I return in a single dream;
Seeking the traces of former days and grieving for men now gone.
Heaven allows our hearts desire, but yields only hindrance to our lives.
A terrace by a pond that awaits the moon, on a river that flows to no
 avail;
A storeyed pavilion that shades the blossoms from the heedless sunset
 glow ....
I climb and gaze with no regard for my ever damper robes.

LI. To "San T'ai Ling" (I)

tš'ün	šêk				
tš'ün	šêk				
.i	ghiu-	ts'ing	mun	tsɨ:	mêk
rit	zhia	liu:	.am-	xwa	.ien
tsüi-	nguâ-	žhui	kya	šiau-	nien
nien	šiau-				
nien	šiau-				
xhying	lak	drhik	süê	ghip	tsau:

Beauty of spring,
Beauty of spring;
Green Gate and Purple Boulevards abide unchanged....
The sun sets on darkened willows and graceful blossoms;
Lying drunk, some lad at the age of youthful bloom.
Bloom of youth,
Bloom of youth,
In pursuit of pleasure, all that counts is catching it in time!

Green Gate: one of the gates of the T'ang capital, Ch'ang-an; it was known in particular as a place of farewell. Purple Boulevards: an elegant term for the streets of the capital.

LII. To "San T'ai Ling" (II)

ming	ngüat				
ming	ngüat				
tšiau-	têk	li	rin	džhêu	dzhüat
kyêng-	šim	.ing:	rip	k'ong	džhwang
put	dhau-	üi	bhying	yia-	drhiang
drhiang	yia-				
drhiang	yia-				
mong-	tau-	dhing	xwa	.im	xhya-

Moonlight,
Moonlight,
Shining a faraway wanderer on to utmost sorrow.
Ever deeper, moonbeams come to her empty bed,
Hard to bear, behind curtains and screens, a night so long....
Long nights,
Long nights,
Dreams until the garden blossoms are deep within the shade.

LIII. To "San T'ai Ling" (III)

nam	p'uê:				
nam	p'uê:				
ts'üi-	pyin-	li	rin	xhâ	tš'iê-
tang	žhi	xhyüi	šiu:	kau	lêu
.i	ghiu-	lêu	dzhien	šüi:	liu
liu	šüi:				
liu	šüi:				
triong	iu:	šiang	sim	šwang	lüi-

South Cove,
South Cove,
Where has my raven-haired faraway wanderer gone?
In times gone by, hand in hand on a tall pavilion....
Abiding unchanged, below the pavilion a river flows.
Flows a river,
Flows a river,
Full of tears that come from an aching heart.

South Cove: since the *Ch'u Tz'u* ("Songs of the South") a conventional name for the home of a beautiful girl.

LIV. To "Tien Chiang Ch'un"

.im-	lüok	üi	xhong			
mong-	ghyüng	kya	dzhai-	dhau	ngüen	drhüê-
xhwa-	ghiau	tang	luê-			
lim	šüi:	šwang	tšüê	xhuê-		

liu:	kying-	tš'ün	šim	
xhying	tau-	kwan	dzhing	tš'iê-
bhyin	put	ngiê-		
.i-	bhing	fung	siê-	
tš'üi	xiang-	lang	pyien	k'iê-

Shaded in green, wrapped in pink,
Dreaming Jewel lives in a house by Peach Blossom Spring.
A painted bridge faces the road;
Overlooking the stream stands a pair of vermilion gates.

On willow pathways deep in springtime,
She walks as far as the place where her heart is touched;
Frowning, mute,
Her thoughts would trouble the wind-borne catkins
To blow her away in her lover's direction.

Dreaming Jewel: Feng Yen-ssu used "jewel" as part of a girl's name in another lyric (not translated here). This has led to speculation that he may have known a girl with this name and that it is to her that the poems refer.
Peach Blossom Spring: In the fifth year of the Yung-p'ing period, during the reign of Emperor Ming of the Han (A.D.62), Liu Ch'en (or Sheng) and Juan Chao, natives of Shan-hsien, went into the area of Mt. T'ien-t'ai together to gather bark and became lost. After ten days, they still had not found their way back. When their provisions were all gone, and they were about to collapse from hunger, they saw on top of a distant hill a peach tree heavily laden with fruit. But there was no trail up to it past the sheer cliffs and deep canyons, and they were only able to reach it by pulling themselves up through the vines. Once they had eaten a few of the peaches, their hunger

was eased and their bodies restored. After they had gotten back down, they went with a cup to get water in order to wash up and rinse their mouths. Just then they saw a turnip leaf—and a very freshly picked one, at that—come floating out through a gap in the hill, followed by a cup with some sesame seed paste in it. "We can't be far from human habitation now!" they exclaimed, as they made their way out into a broad glen. At its edge, they found two young women of breathtaking charm and beauty. As soon as the latter saw the two of them emerging with the cup, they laughed and said, "Mr. Liu and Mr. Juan have caught the cup we set afloat!" Although Ch'en and Chao didn't recognize them, the two girls called them by name as though they were old acquaintances, delighted to see them and asking why they were so late, since it was almost time to go home. Their home had a tile roof, and along the north and east walls were large beds, both decorated with red gauze curtains, hung with bells at the corners and ornamented with filigree work in gold and silver above. At the head of each bed stood ten maid servants, who stepped forward and said, "Mr. Liu and Mr. Juan, you have crossed the impenetrable mountains and come west to obtain the precious fruit. If you can accept our poor fare, we can prepare a meal quickly." There was sesame-rice and goat's meat, both quite delicious. When the meal was over, wine was brought in, and a crowd of girls arrived, each bringing a few peaches. They laughed and said, "We have come to congratulate you on your new husbands, to drink and make merry!" Liu and Juan were both delighted and alarmed by this. When evening fell, each was directed to one of the curtained beds, where he was joined by one of the girls. Their voices were so pure and gentle that they made one forget all his troubles. But after ten days had passed, the men began to think about returning home. Then the girls said, "Your coming here was at the command of your good fortune. After being accepted by fairy maidens, what pleasure could you find in the common world?" And so they remained for half a year, during which time the weather was always like that of late spring. Ch'en and Chao could not get over their wish to go home. Since the girls were daughters of the King of Fairies, they finally gathered thirty people to play music and bid them farewell, showing them the road back: When they got out, they found their families and friends all gone and their villages and houses completely changed and beyond recognition. They were able to locate one of their descendants in the seventh generation, who told them that he had heard of their going into the hills, getting lost, and never returning (Liu Yi-ch'ing, *Yu-ming Lu*, 16ab).

The NAN-T'ANG ERH-CHU TZ'U

I. To "Ying T'ien Ch'ang"

.yit	kêu	tš'ê	ngüat	lim	tšwang	king-
žhien	pyin-	vhung-	tš'ai	žhüong	put	tšing:
drhüong	liam	dzhing-				
dzhêng	lêu	xhyüng-				
tr'iu	tr'iang-	lak	xwa	fung	put	dhing-
liu:	ti	fang	ts'au:	kying-		
mong-	dhuan-	lok	luê	kim	tsing:	
dzhak	yia-	kyêng	lan	tsiu:	sing:	
tš'ün	džhêu	kuâ	k'iak	bhing-		

Just a hook, the new moon looks down on a dressing mirror;
Cicada hairdress and phoenix pins left heedlessly awry.
Doubled blinds are still;
The storeyed pavilion remote;
Mournful and forlorn, falling blossoms the wind will not let rest.
On willow banks the paths through fragrant grass,
A dream is broken by the windlass of a decorated well....
Last night as the watches ended, awakening from wine,
Spring sorrow worse than any illness.

II. To "Wang Yuan Hsing"

.

pik	ts'i-	xwa	kuang	kim:	siu-	ming
tšüê	fyi	drhiang	rit	trin	drhiang	kyüng
yia-	xhan	put	k'iê-	mong-	nan	žhing
luê	xiang	.yien	lêng:	dzhɨ-	dhing	dhing

liau	yiang	ngüat				
muat	ling	trim				
put	drhüen	siau	sik	dhan-	drhüen	dzhing
xhuang	kim	tš'wang	xhya-	xut	rien	king
tšing	rin	küi	rit	ri-	muau	šêng

On jade steps the glow of blossoms is bright as brocade, embroidery;
My vermilion gate remains securely barred all day long.
The chill of night will not depart, dreams are hard to complete;
Cold smoke from an incense burner floats up in a thin stream.

The moon above Liao-yang,
The washing stones of Mo-ling,
Convey no news, convey only sadness.
Below a golden window I am suddenly shaken—
When my wanderer comes home I shall be old and grey.

Liao-yang: a place in southern Manchuria, in the area of the modern city of the same name.
During the early years of the T'ang dynasty, there was a series of campaigns against the Koreans
and other frontier peoples in this area. As casualties were heavy and communications poor,
Liao-yang came to stand for distant and prolonged absence with little prospect of return.
Mo-ling: an old name for Chin-ling (Nanking), the capital city of Southern T'ang.

III. To "Huan Hsi Sha"

šiu:	küan:	tšin	tšüê	žhiang-	ngüok	kêu
.i	dzhien	tš'ün	xhên-	suâ:	drhüong	lêu
fung	li:	lak	xwa	žhüi	žhi-	tšüê:
si-	yiu	yiu				

ts'ing	tiau:	put	drhüen	ün	nguai-	sin-
ting	xiang	k'ong	kyiat	üê:	triong	džhêu
xhuai	šiu:	lüok	puâ	sam	tš'ê:	muê-
tsiap	t'ien	liu				

My hands have rolled the beaded blinds up to their hooks of jade;
Just as before, the heart-ache of spring is locked in a storeyed pavilion.
Falling blossoms borne by the wind—who will see to them?
Thoughts long and brooding.

Black birds bring me no word from beyond the clouds;
Wisteria blossoms knot my sorrow in the rain to no avail.
I look back toward the green waves of twilight over Ch'u,
Flowing on to touch the sky.

Black birds: See the note to Feng Yen-ssu, poem VII.
Ch'u: the middle Yangtse valley region, roughly the modern provinces of Hupei and Hunan.

IV. To "Huan Hsi Sha"

xham-	dham-	xiang	siau	ts'üi-	yiap	dzhan
si	fung	džhêu	k'i:	lüok	puâ	kyan
xhwan	yiê:	yüong	kuang	ghüong-	dzhiau	dzhüi-
put	k'am	k'an				

si-	üê:	mong-	xhuai	kyi	sai-	üan:
siau:	lêu	tš'üi	drhiat	ngüok	šêng	xhan
tâ	šiau:	lüi-	tšüê	xhâ	xhyan-	xhên-
.i:	lan	kan				

Lotus blossoms' fragrance fades, their raven leaves decay;
A west wind arises sadly among the green waves.
As though to make my features too grow weary and haggard....
I cannot bear to look.

In fine rain my dreams return to far away Chi-sai;
Done playing in a tiny pavilion, the cold of jade pipes.
How many teardrop pearls, what end to my heart-ache,
As I lean against a railing?

Chi-sai ("Cock Fort"): usually identified with various places on the Mongolian frontier, with connotations rather like those of Liao-yang in poem II. A recent but inconclusive exchange between two Japanese scholars, Takeuchi Teruo and Fukumoto Masakazu, has raised the possibility that it may refer instead to a pond in the hills near Nanking (Fukumoto) or to an actual enclosure for chickens, whose morning crowing ends the dream (Takeuchi).

V. To "Yü Mei-jen"

tšʼün	xwa	tsʼiu	ngüat	xhâ	žhi	liau:		
üang:	žhɨ-	tri	tâ	šiau:				
siau:	lêu	dzhak	yia-	iu-	tong	fung		
kuê-	kuk	put	kʼam	xhuai	šiu:	ngüat	ming	triong

tiau	lan	ngüok	tsʼi-	.i	rien	dzhai-		
tši	žhɨ-	tšüê	ngyan	kai:				
vun-	kün	tuê	iu:	ki:	tâ	džhêu		
kʼyap	zhɨ-	.yit	kyang	tšʼün	šüi:	xiang-	tong	liu

Spring flowers, the moon in autumn, when will these cease to be?
So many things lie already in the past.
Last night to my tiny pavilion the east wind came again;
I could not bear to look back toward my old kingdom shining beneath
the moon.

Carved railings and jade-paved ways must be there just the same;
My rosy cheeks alone have changed.
Ask the sum of sorrow, ask how much there is to bear;
Just what is borne by a river in full spring flood flowing eastward
to the sea.

For a discussion of the meaning of "rosy cheeks" in this poem, and in poem XXIV, see Lai Wood-yan, "Li Yü Chi-chung 'Juan Lang Kuei' yü 'Yü Mei-jen.'"

VI. To "Wu Yeh T'i"

dzhak	yia-	fung	kyiam	üê:		
liam	üi	sap	sap	ts'iu	šing	
tšuok	dzhan	lêu-	tik	bhyin	.i	tšim:
k'i:	dzhuâ-	put	nêng	bhing		

ši-	žhɨ-	muan-	zhüi	liu	šüi:	
suan	lai	mong-	li:	vhu	šêng	
tsüi-	xiang	luê-	.un:	ngi	bhyin	tau-
ts'ɨ:	nguai-	put	k'am	xhying		

Yesterday evening wind joined with the rain;
And blinds and curtains rustled and sighed with an autumn sound.
As candles burnt out and clocks ran down I tossed and turned on my
   pillow;
Getting up and lying down again I found no peace.

The things of this world heedlessly follow the flowing river,
And count for no more than the drifting life in a dream.
The roads of Drunken Land are smooth, and there should I often go,
For there are no others that I can bear to walk.

Drunken Land: The Early T'ang poet Wang Chi wrote a short essay called "A Record of Drunken
Land." See his collected works, *Tung-kao-tzu Chi*, C.7a–8a. There is a translation by Herbert
A. Giles, in *Gems of Chinese Literature*, 1:111–12.

VII. To "Yi Hu Chu"

xyiau:	tšwang	tš'ê	kuâ-			
drhim	dhan	k'ying	tšüê-	sia	ri	kâ-
xiang-	rin	vyi	luê-	ting	xiang	k'uâ:
.yit	k'üok	ts'ing	kâ			
dzham-	yin:	.ying	dhau	p'uâ-		

lâ	zhiu-	.ip	dzhan	.yan	šêk	k'â:
puai	šim	zhüen	bhi-	xiang	lau	.uâ-
siu-	džhwang	zhia	bhing-	kiau	vuê	nâ-
lan-	dzhiak	xhong	riong			
siau-	xiang-	dhan	lang	t'uâ-		

Morning adornment finished now,
She dabs a few drops of aloes and sandalwood here and there;
Giving her lover just a glimpse of a tiny wisteria kernel,
With a single song in her clear voice
It breaks teasingly for a moment between cherry blossom lips.

Gossamer sleeves are slightly damp with scattered crimson stains;
The depths of her cup are gradually soiled by a layer of fragrant lees.
She leans across her embroidered bed, bewitchingly coy and languid,
Chewing to pulp a scarlet thread
And spitting it with a playful smile at her Master Sandalwood.

Aloes and sandalwood were used in making both scents and colouring for women's eyebrows.
Master Sandalwood: a nickname given to the poet P'an Yüeh (d.300) who, as a young man, was
so handsome that women found him irresistable.

VIII. To "Tzu-yeh Ko"

rin	šêng	džhêu	xhên-	xhâ	nêng	mian:
siau	xhun	dhok	ngâ:	dzhing	xhâ	xhyan-
kuê-	kuk	mong-	drhüong	küi		
kyak	lai	šwang	lüi-	žhüi		

kau	lêu	žhüi	yiê:	žhiang:
drhiang	ki-	ts'iu	dzhing	vang-
üang:	žhɨ-	yi:	žhing	k'ong
xhwan	riê	.yit	mong-	triong

No one can be spared the sorrow and heart-ache of human life;
Am I alone so overwhelmed, what end does my sadness have?
To my former kingdom returning in dreams again,
I awaken to find my tears already brimming.

With whom did I climb the tall pavilions then?
I will always remember gazing at the clear autumn sky.
Bygone days are past and turned to nothing,
As though they were moments within a single dream.

IX. To "Keng-lou-tzu"

(this poem is by Wen T'ing-yün; see Appendix B)

X. To "Lin-Chiang Hsien"

.ying	dhau	lak	dzhin-	tš'ün	küi	k'iê-
dhiap	fan	k'ying	fun:	šwang	fyi	
tsɨ:	kyüi	dhi	ngüat	siau:	lêu	si
ngüok	kêu	lâ	mak			
tr'iu	tr'iang-	muê-	.yien	žhüi		

bhiat	xhyang-	dzhik	liau	rin	san-	xhêu-
vang-	dzhan	.yien	ts'au:	ti	myi	
luê	xiang	xhyan	niau:	vhung-	xhuang	ri
k'ong	drhi	lâ	tai-			
xhuai	šiu:	xhên-	.i	.i		

All ended, the fall of cherry blossoms—spring has gone away;
Butterflies float by in pairs on light fluttering wings.
A nighthawk calls out to the moon west of a tiny pavilion;
From jade hooks, my gossamer curtains
Hang mournful and forlorn in twilight mist.

The farewell lane is still and empty now that all are gone;
Vacantly I gaze across the dim and hazy meadow.
Incense rises gently from a censer in little phoenix coils;
Holding for nothing a gossamer sash,
I look back, and heart-ache lingers on.

I accept as genuine the last three lines of this poem, which are not found in the *Nan-T'ang Erh-chu Tz'u* but were published in a version of the poem that appeared somewhat later in Ch'en Hu's *Ch'i-chiu Hsü-wen*, 3.4a. See my "The 'Hsieh Hsin En' Fragments."

XIa. To "Wang Chiang-nan"

tâ	šiau:	xhên-				
dzhak	yia-	mong-	xhun	triong		
xhwan	zhɨ-	ghiu-	žhi	yiu	žhiang-	.üan:
kiê	riê	liu	šüi:	ma:	riê	lüong
xwa	ngüat	tšing-	tš'ün	fung		

So much heart-ache:
Last night my soul within a dream
Seemed again, as in days gone by, to roam the Palace Gardens—
Carriages like a flowing river, horses like a dragon,
And blossoms and moonlight just in the mood of spring.

XIb. To "Wang Chiang-nan"

tâ	šiau:	lüi-				
dhuan-	lam:	vhuk	xhwêng	yi		
sim	žhɨ-	mak	tsiang	xhuâ	lüi-	šüat
vhung-	šêng	xiu	xiang-	lüi-	žhi	tš'üi
drhiang	dhuan-	kyêng-	vuê	ngi		

So many tears:
They stain your cheeks and run down across your chin;
Better not to tell with flowing tears the sorrows of your heart,
And neither should you play your phoenix pipes as tears come on,
For surely then your heart would break in two.

XII. To "Ch'ing-p'ing Yüeh"

bhiat	lai	tš'ün	puan-			
tš'üok	mok	džhêu	drhiang	dhuan-		
ts'i-	xhya-	lak	muai	riê	süat	luan-
fut	liau:	.yit	šin	xhwan	muan:	

ngyan-	lai	.im	sin-	vuê	bhing	
luê-	yiau	küi	mong-	nan	žhing	
li	xhên-	k'yap	riê	tš'ün	ts'au:	
kyêng-	xhying	kyêng-	üan:	xhwan	šêng	

Since our parting, spring is half gone;
Everything I see brings heart-rending sorrow.
Below the steps the falling plum blossoms whirl like snow,
No sooner brushed away than drifting over again.

In news conveyed by migrating geese I have no faith;
The road is so long that dreams of return cannot reach home.
The heart-ache of separation is like the new grass of springtime:
No matter how you wander, no matter how far—and still it grows.

XIII. To "Ts'ai Sang-tzu"

dhing	dzhien	tš'ün	drhiok	xhong	.ing	dzhin-
vuê:	t'ai-	bhuai	xhuai			
si-	üê:	fyi	vyi			
put	fang-	šwang	mi	žhi	dzham-	k'ai

lüok	tš'wang	lêng:	dzhing-	fang	.im	dhuan-
xiang	.yin-	žhing	xuai			
k'â:	nai-	dzhing	xhwai			
yüok	žhüi-	mong	long	rip	mong-	lai

Before the arbour, spring hastens the scarlet blossoms all away;
To and fro they whirl and dance.
In a fine mist of drizzling rain,
I cannot relax my knitted brows even for a moment.

The green window is cold and still, your fragrant letters have ceased;
Incense cakes turn slowly to ashes.
Unable to endure the longing in my heart—
But as I drift drowsily to sleep, you come into my dreams.

XIV. To "Hsi Ch'ien Ying"

```
xyiau:    ngüat    drhüi-
siok      ün       vyi
vuê       ngiê:    tšim:    bhyin    .i
mong-     xhuai    fang     ts'au:   si-      .i      .i
t'ien     üan:     ngyan-   šing     xi

dhi       .ying    san-
yiê       xwa      luan-
dzhik     mak      xhwa-    dhang    šim      üan-
p'yian-   xhong    xiu      sau:     dzhin-   dzhüong  .yi
liu       dhai-    vuê:     rin      küi
```

The daybreak moon descends;
Clouds of night thin out;
Mute and restless I toss upon my pillow.
My dreams return to fragrant herbs, thoughts that linger on;
The heavens are far, the cries of wild geese few.

Singing warblers scatter;
Remnant blossoms whirl;
Still and forlorn the long courtyard and painted halls.
Do not sweep away the petals of scarlet, leave them be
Where they lie to await the dancers' coming home.

Aoyama Hiroshi has devoted an article to the expression "dreams return"; see his "Tō-Sō Shi ni Okeru 'Mukai' no Go."

XV. To "Tieh Lien Hua"

yiau	yia-	dhing	kau	xhyan	sin-	bhuê-
džha-	kuâ-	ts'ing	ming			
tsau:	kyak	šiang	tš'ün	muê-		
šuê-	tiam:	üê:	šing	fung	.iak	drhüê-
mong	long	dham-	ngüat	ün	lai	k'iê-

dhau	li:	.i	.i	tš'ün	.am-	dhuê-
žhüi	dzhai-	ts'iu	ts'ien			
siau-	li:	ti	ti	ngiê-		
.yit	p'yian-	fang	sim	ts'ien	van-	zhįê-
rin	kyan	mut	kâ-	.an	bhai	tš'iê-

A leisurely evening in garden and meadow—I follow my idle footsteps;
The Ch'ing-ming Holiday almost over
Makes me ache already for the waning of spring.
A few drops—the sound of rain held in check by the wind;
Dim and hazy under a pale moon the clouds come and go.

As blossoming peaches lingered on, spring passed by in secret;
But who is sitting in the swing,
Laughing softly and whispering quiet and low?
A single bit of fragrant heart, a million trailing threads;
In the world of men there is no place to arrange them all in peace.

XVI. To "Wu Yeh T'i"

lim	xwa	zhia-	liau:	tš'ün	xhong			
t'ai-	ts'ong	ts'ong						
žhiang	xhên-	triau	lai	xhan	üê:	van:	lai	fung

.yien	tši	lüi-						
liu	rin	tsüi-						
ki:	žhi	drhüong						
dzhɨ-	žhi-	rin	šêng	drhiang	xhên-	šüi:	drhiang	tong

Forest blossoms have now relinquished their springtime scarlet,
All too hurriedly;
My constant sorrow, the cold rain of morning, the wind of evening.

Tears of pink rouge
Keep us drinking together,
For when shall we meet again?
Such the eternal sorrows of human life, rivers' eternal eastward flow.

XVII. To "Ch'ang Hsiang-ssu"

ün	.yit	kuâ				
ngüok	.yit	suâ				
dham-	dham-	šam	ri	bhak	bhak	lâ
k'ying	bhyin	šwang	dhai-	luâ		

ts'iu	fung	tâ	.			
üê:	siang	xhuâ				
liam	nguai-	pa	tsiau	sam	liang:	k'uâ
yia-	drhiang	rin	nai-	xhâ		

A single swirl of cloud,
A single shuttle of jade;
A pale, pale bodice of thin, thin gossamer,
A slightly knitted pair of painted brows....

Heavy, the autumn winds,
And joined with them the rain;
Outside the blinds, a stand of several banana trees....
As nights grow long, what am I to do?

XVIII. To "Tao Lien-tzu Ling"

šim	üan-	dzhing-				
siau:	dhing	k'ong				
dhuan-	zhüok	xhan	trim	dhuan-	zhüok	fung
vuê	nai-	yia-	drhiang	rin	put	myi-
šuê-	šing	xhuâ	ngüat	tau-	liam	long

The long courtyard is still,
The tiny garden deserted;
Now and then, cold washing stones, now and then the wind....
Who could endure a night so long, unable to sleep,
The various sounds that join the moonbeams in coming through
   latticed blinds?

XIX. To "Huan Hsi Sha"

xhong	rit	yi:	kau	sam	drhiang-	t'êu-
kim	luê	ts'ɨ-	dhi-	t'iam	xiang	šiu-
xhong	kim:	dhi-	.i	zhüi	bhuê-	tšêu-
kya	rin	vuê:	tiam:	kim	tš'ai	liu-
tsiu:	.ak	žhi	niam	xwa	rüi:	xiu-
bhiat	dhian-	yiau	vun	siau	kuê:	tsêu-

The red sun has risen now and filters in from high above;
Golden censers are filled by turns with incense in animal forms,
And rugs of red brocade are wrinkled by idly passing steps.
Beautiful women are dancing in time, their golden pins slip loose,
As I, sick with wine, pinch off and sniff the scented flower stamens
Hearing in the distance flutes and drums perform in another palace.

Robert van Gulik (*Sexual Life in Ancient China*, p. 214, n.1, with an additional reference to p. 107) understands the animal shape to be that of the incense burner. That such utensils were common is well known, and van Gulik is quite right to point out that they are the usual meaning of *hsiang-shou*. But Hoffmann, to whose translation (*Die Lieder des Li Yü*, p. 25), van Gulik is objecting, Chan An-t'ai (*Li Ching Li Yü Tz'u*, p. 14), and Murakami (*Ri Iku*, p. 33) all understand the meaning of the term in this poem to be "incense in animal shape," and the latter explains that the confusion is the result of a reversal of normal word order for the sake of a rhyme.

XX. To "P'u-sa Man"

xwa	ming	ngüat	.am-	long	k'ying	vuê-
kim	triau	xau:	xiang-	lang	pyien	k'iê-
tš'an:	vat	bhuê-	xiang	kyai		
šiu:	dhi	kim	lüê:	xhyai		

xhwa-	dhang	nam	bhuan-	kyian-
.yit	xiang-	.uai	rin	tšian-
nuê	üi-	tš'üt	lai	nan
kyau	kün	tsɨ-	.i-	lien

Blossoms bright and moonlight dim, veiled by a trace of fog;
Now is the perfect chance to steal away to her lover's side.
Stockinged footsteps tread the fragrant stairs;
Held in hand, her gold-sewn shoes.

They meet by the south of a painted hall,
And she trembles for a moment in his nestling arms;
"Because it is so hard for me to come out,
I urge you now to indulge your deepest love!"

XXIa. To "Wang Chiang Mei"

xhyan	mong-	üan:				
nam	kuk	tšing-	fang	tš'ün		
žhüen	žhiang-	kuan:	xhyien	kyang	myian-	lüok
muan:	žhing	fyi	siê-	kun:	k'ying	drhin
mang	šai-	k'an-	xwa	rin		

My idle dreams are far away
In a southern land at the height of fragrant spring:
Boats are laden with flutes and strings on the surface of green rivers,
A city flooded with floating catkins mixed in a haze of dust,
And people rushing out to see the blossoms.

XXIb. To "Wang Chiang Mei"

xhyan	mong-	üan:				
nam	kuk	tšing-	ts'ing	ts'iu		
ts'ien	li:	kyang	šan	xhan	šêk	üan:
luê	xwa	šim	tš'iê-	bhak	kuê	tšiu
dhik	dzhai-	ngüat	ming	lêu		

My idle dreams are far away
In a southern land at the height of clear autumn:
In hills and rivers a thousand leagues distant, cold colours far away;
Deep among the flowering rushes a solitary boat is moored,
And flutes resound in moonbright towers.

XXII. To "P'u-sa Man"

bhong	lai	üan-	pyi-	t'ien	t'ai	nriê:
xhwa-	dhang	triu-	ts'im:	rin	vuê	ngiê:
p'au	tšim:	ts'üi-	ün	kuang		
siu-	.i	vun	yi-	xiang		

dzhiam	lai	tšüê	suâ:	dhong-
king	kyak	ngin	bhying	mong-
lam:	muan-	siau-	ying	ying
siang	k'an	vuê	xhyan-	dzhing

On P'eng-lai Isle a courtyard encloses a girl from Mt. T'ien-t'ai;
In a painted hall she sleeps in silence through the day.
Thrown over her pillow, the sheen of a raven cloud;
On embroidered robes is scented a strange fragrance.

Stealthily entering—a pearl latch stirs;
She awakens with a start from a dream of silver screens....
Slowly her face overflows with smiles of joy,
As she gazes upon him with boundless love.

P'eng-lai Isle: a magic island supposed to lie in the sea to the east of China.
T'ien-t'ai: a mountain in Chekiang, supposedly the site of an encounter with two fairy women at
Peach Blossom Spring; see Feng Yen-ssu, poem LIV.

XXIII. To "P'u-sa Man"

dhong	xhuang	ün-	ts'üi-	ts'iang	xhan	triok
sin	šing	muan-	tsêu-	yi	siam	ngüok
ngyan:	šêk	.am-	siang	kêu		
ts'iu	puâ	xhwêng-	yüok	liu		

üê:	ün	šim	siu-	xhuê-
vyi-	bhyian-	xhyai	triong	suê-
.yian-	bha-	iu-	žhing	k'ong
mong-	myi	tš'ün	üê:	triong

Brass reeds in crisp concord, the clatter of cold bamboo,
A new song slowly performed by moving slender jade.
Flashing eyes offer secret enticement,
And autumn ripples begin to surge and flow.

Clouds and rain within deep embroidered doors;
Never a chance to confide one's deepest feelings.
The banquet is over; all is empty again,
As dreams go astray among the rains of spring.

XXIV. To "Juan Lang Kuei"

tong	fung	tš'üi	šüi:	rit	xhyam	šan
tš'ün	lai	drhiang	žhi-	xhyan		
lak	xwa	lang	dzhik	tsiu:	lan	san
šêng	kâ	tsüi-	mong-	kyan		

bhuai-	šing	ts'iau:				
van:	tšwang	dzhan				
bhing	žhüi	tšing:	ts'üi-	xhwan		
liu	lien	kuang	king:	sik	tšüê	ngyan
xhuang	xun	dhok	.i:	lan		

An east wind blows over the river, the sun is nestled in the hills;
Since spring has come, our idle leisure is unbroken.
Fallen blossoms are tattered and torn, the banquet in full swing;
Pipes and singing among our drunken dreams.

Rustling ornaments stilled,
Evening powder faded,
On whose account does she straighten her raven tresses?
There in the lingering radiant glow, pitying her rosy cheeks,
She leans alone against a railing in the yellow twilight.

Wang Cheng-wen (pp. 36–38) discusses at length the attribution of this poem to Feng Yen-ssu, which he is inclined to credit.

XXV. To "Lang T'ao Sha"

üang:	žhi-	tši	k'am	.ai		
tuai-	king:	nan	bhai			
ts'iu	fung	dhing	üan-	sian:	ts'im	kyai
.yit	xhang	tšüê	liam	xhyan	put	küan:
tšiong	rit	žhüi	lai			

kim	küam-	yi:	drhim	mai		
tšwang-	k'i-	xau	lai			
van:	liang	t'ien	dzhing-	ngüat	xhwa	k'ai
siang:	têk	ngüok	lêu	yiau	dhian-	.ing:
k'ong	tšiau-	dzhin	xhwai			

Bygone times may only be lamented;
They appear before me, hard to put to rest.
An autumn wind blows in the gardens and lichen invades the stairs;
A single row of beaded blinds hangs idly down unrolled,
As no one comes the whole day through.

My golden sabre now lies buried deep;
My youthful spirit is turned to weeds.
In the cool of evening, the heavens are still and the moon blossoms forth;
I call to mind the jade pavilions, the reflected nephrite halls,
Glowing empty in the River Ch'in-huai.

Ch'in-huai: a small stream that flows along the southern edges of Nanking; it was an elegant district during the Southern Dynasties (317–589).

XXVI. To "Ts'ai Sang-tzu"

lok	luê	kim	tsing:	nguê	dhong	van:
ki	žhüê-	king	ts'iu			
triu-	üê:	sin	džhêu			
pêk	tš'ik	xhya	süê	dzhai-	ngüok	kêu

ghyüng	tš'wang	mong-	dhuan-	šwang	ngâ	tšêu-
xhuai	šiu:	pyien	dhêu			
yüok	ki-	lin	yiu			
kiu:	k'üok	xhan	puâ	put	suê-	liu

Phoenix trees by the windlass of a decorated well in evening,
A few boughs ashiver with autumn.
Rain during the day brings new sorrow;
A hundred feet up hang shrimp-whisker blinds on jade hooks.

In a jewel window spring is sundered—moth eyebrows furrow....
Turning to look toward the distant frontier,
She longs to send word by a roaming fish,
But the wintry waves of the Nine Meanders will not turn back their flow.

Shrimp-whisker blinds: a kind of rattan blind made of very thin strips.
Nine Meanders: a reference to the nine changes of direction in the Yellow River on its way from
the northwestern frontier area to the sea.

XXVII. To "Yü Mei-jen"

fung	xhuai	siau:	üan-	dhing	vuê	lüok		
liu:	ngyan:	tš'ün	siang	zhüok				
bhing-	lan	puan-	rit	dhok	vuê	ngien		
.i	ghiu-	triok	šing	sin	ngüat	zhɨ-	tang	nien

šêng	kâ	vyi-	san-	tsun	dzhien	dzhai-		
drhi	myian-	ping	tš'ê	kyai:				
tšüok	ming	xiang	.am-	xhwa-	dhang	šim		
muan:	pyin-	ts'ing	šwang	dzhan	süat	sɨ-	nan	rim

Breezes eddy in a tiny courtyard, garden weeds turn green;
Willows in bud bring springtime in its turn.
Leaning on a railing half the day, silent and alone—
Abiding unchanged, the sound of bamboo and the new moon, just as
  in years gone by.

Pipes and singing not yet dismissed, winecups remain before us;
The ice on the pond has just begun to break up.
The glow of candles is dimmed by incense in the depth of a painted hall;
My temples covered with clear frost and patches of snow—thoughts
  hard to bear....

XXVIII. To "Yü Lou Ch'un"

van:	tšwang	tš'ê	liau:	ming	ki	süat
tš'ün	dhian-	p'yin	ngâ	ngiê	kuan-	liat
šêng	siau	tš'üi	dhuan-	šüi:	ün	kyan
drhüong	.an-	ngyi	žhiang	kâ	pyian-	drhiat

lim	tš'ün	žhüi	kyêng-	p'yiau	xiang	siat
tsüi-	p'êk	lan	kan	dzhing	vyi-	ts'iat
küi	žhi	xiu	tšiau-	tšüok	xwa	xhong
dhai-	fang-	ma:	dhi	ts'ing	yia-	ngüat

Evening makeup finished now, bright skin snow white,
The Spring Palace consorts and maids line up like schools of fish.
The playing of pipes and flutes fills the void between river and clouds,
As once again they play to the end the Song of Rainbow Skirts.

Who in Viewing Spring now sets these slips of fragrance adrift?
Drunkenly beating on the railings, the flavour in my heart is keen.
As I return, leave no candle blossoms glowing red;
I shall give free rein to my horse's stride in the clear moonlit night.

The Song of Rainbow Skirts: a famous piece of music from the T'ang dynasty; it had been almost
forgotten by Li Yü's time, but his wife Chao-hui is said to have restored it on the basis of a tat-
tered and incomplete copy of the score. This is referred to in the "Dirge" that he wrote after her
death; see Appendix A.
Viewing Spring: name of a pavilion that housed the favoured consort of the last Emperor of the
Ch'en dynasty (sixth century).

XXIX. To "Tzu-yeh Ko"

zhim	tš'ün	süê	žhi-	sien	tš'ün	tsau:
k'an	xwa	mak	dhai-	xwa	tši	lau:
p'yiau:	šêk	ngüok	riu	ghing		
p'uai	vhu	tšan:	myian-	ts'ing		

xhâ	fang	bhyin	siau-	ts'an-
kim-	.üan:	tš'ün	küi	van:
dhong	tsüi-	yiê:	xhyan	bhing
ši	zhüi	kiat	kuê:	žhing

In seeking spring, it must be now while spring is early;
In viewing blossoms, do not wait for the blossomed boughs to age.
Pale green coloured jade is delicately raised,
And new wine glistens clear in brimming bowls.

What objection to hearty laughter at our feast
In the Forbidden Garden while spring lingers still?
Drunk together we join in casual comments
As poems are finished to the beat of a nomad drum.

XXX. To "Hsieh Hsin En"

kim   tš'wang   lik   k'un-   k'i: xhwan   žhüong

Weary in a golden window, but rising, listless yet.

Poems XXX–XXXV were added to the *Nan-T'ang Erh-chu Tz'u* from what was evidently a badly damaged manuscript. I have discussed my resolution of the many textual problems they present elsewhere, in the article "The 'Hsieh Hsin En' Fragments." The only other serious attempt to deal with the textual dilemmas is that of Mizuhara Ikō (Nan-Tō Goshu, Pt. 2, pp. 58–59), whose suggestions are much less detailed.

XXXI. To "Hsieh Hsin En"

dzhin	lêu	put	kyian-	tš'üi	siau	nriê:
k'ong	yiê	žhiang-	.üan:	fung	kuang	
fun:	.ing	kim	rüi:	dzhɨ-	ti	ngang
tong	fung	nau:	ngâ:			
dzhai	fat	.yit	kim	xiang		

ghyüng	tš'wang	mong-	[...]	liu	dzhan	rit
tang	nien	têk	xhên-	xhâ	drhiang	
pik	lan	kan	nguai-	.ing-	žhüi	yiang
dzham-	žhi	siang	kyian-			
riê	mong-	lan:	sɨ	liang		

In the pavilions of Ch'in the girl who played her flute is nowhere to
    be seen;
To no avail remains the beauty of the Palace Gardens.
Powdery blossoms and golden stamens wave high and low;
The east wind torments me,
Bringing with it just a breath of fragrance.

Dreams of a jewel window [...] the last of day remains;
How long will I suffer heart-ache for bygone years?
Beyond balustrades of jade, trailing willows glow;
I met you once, and only for a moment,
As though in a dream, I hesitate to think it through.

Hsiao Shih lived at the time of Duke Mu of Ch'in (r.658–20 B.C.). He was an excellent performer
on the flute and could attract peacocks and cranes into his garden. Duke Mu had a daughter
named Nung-yü. She fell in love with Hsiao, and so the Duke gave her to him as a wife. He taught
Nung-yü each day to perform the cry of a phoenix, and after some years her playing resembled
a phoenix's song. When a phoenix came and roosted on their roof, the Duke had the Phoenix
Terrace built, and the couple lived in its upper storey without ever coming down. Several years
passed, and then one day they both flew away with the phoenix. On this account, the people of
Ch'in built a shrine to the "Phoenix Girl" in Yung. Sometimes the sound of a flute is heard inside
the shrine wall (Liu Hsiang, *Lieh Hsien Chuan*, A.15ab).

XXXII. To "Hsieh Hsin En"

.ying	xwa	lak	dzhin-	kyai	dzhien	ngüat
zhiang-	džhwang	džhêu	.i:	xün	long	
üan:	žhi-	k'iê-	nien			
kim	rit	xhên-	xhwan	dhong		

šwang	xhwan	put	tšing:	ün	dzhiau	dzhüi-
lüi-	triam	xhong	muat	xüong		
xhâ	tš'iê-	siang	sɨ	k'uê:		
ša	tš'wang	tsüi-	mong-	triong		

All ended, the fall of cherry blossoms on steps beneath the moon;
She leans sadly upon the incense frame beside her ivory bed.
Though the past year seems far away,
Her heart-ache today is still the same.

The paired coils of her hairdo are awry, a cloud weary and haggard;
Tears moisten her scarlet bodice.
Where is it that she feels the bitterness of love?
In drunken dreams within a gauze-lined window.

XXXIIIa. To "Hsieh Hsin En"

dhing	k'ong	k'yêk	san-	rin	küi	xhêu-
xhwa-	dhang	puan-	.iam:	tšüê	liam	
lim	fung	sik	sik	yia-	.yiam	.yiam
siau:	lêu	sin	ngüat			
xhuai	šiu:	dzhɨ-	siam	siam		

Garden empty, guests dispersed, after all the people have gone home,
A painted hall is half closed off by beaded blinds.
The wind in the woods moans and sighs; the night is long and still.
A tiny pavilion, the new moon,
As I look back, such slender grace....

XXXIIIb. To "Hsieh Hsin En"

tš'ün	kuang	trin	dzhai-	rin	k'ong	lau:
sin	džhêu	üang:	xhên-	xhâ	ghiong	
.yit	šing	k'iang	dhik			
king	k'i:	tsüi-	yi	yüong		

The glow of spring will always abide, but men grow old in vain;
Where an end to new sorrows and bygone heart-ache...?
A single note from a nomad flute
Awakens her with a dreamy drunken smile.

XXXIV. To "Hsieh Hsin En"

.ying	xwa	lak	dzhin-	tš'ün	tsiang	k'un-
ts'iu	ts'ien	kya-	xhya-	küi	žhi	
muan:	kyai	zhia	ngüat			
drhi	drhi	xwa	dzhai-	tši		

. . . .
. . . .

drhiat	xyiau:	ša	tš'wang	xhya-
dhai-	lai	kün	put	tri

All ended, the fall of cherry blossoms—spring is almost gone;
But as I return, beneath the swing's frame,
The steps are bathed in slanting moonlight,
And blossoms linger upon the boughs.
                    (two lines missing)
Until dawn beneath my gauze-lined window,
I waited for you, but you did not care.

XXXV. To "Hsieh Hsin En"

riam:	riam:	ts'iu	kuang	liu	put	drhüê-
muan:	kyai	xhong	yiap	muê-		
iu-	žhi-	kuâ	drhüong	yiang		
dhai	zhia-	têng	lim	tš'iê-		
žhüê	yüê	xiang	drhüi-			
tsɨ:	kiok	k'i-	p'yiau			
dhing	xhuê-	van:	.yien	long	si-	üê:
.üong	.üong	sin	ngyan-	.yiat	xhan	šing
džhêu	xhên-	nien	nien	drhiang	siang	zhɨ-

Slowly dwindling, the glow of autumn fades, may not be stayed;
In twilight the steps are covered with scarlet leaves.
Once again we keep the day of Double Nine,
And by terraces and pavilions where one may climb and gaze,
The fragrance of dogwood leaves drifts down
And a breath of lavender chrysanthemums floats
In courtyard gates where evening mist enshrouds the fine rain.
In monotone, the strangled wintry cries of new wild geese,
As year after long year my pain and sorrow remain unchanged.

Mizuhara Ikō would rearrange the text of this poem so as to give the following ("Nan-Tō Goshu," Pt. 2, p. 59):

Slowly dwindling, the glow of autumn fades, may not be stayed;
In twilight the steps are covered with scarlet leaves.
[line missing]
Once again we keep the day of Double Nine,
By terraces and pavilions where one may climb and gaze.
[stanza break]
In monotone, the strangled wintry cries of new wild geese,
As year after year ["long" is omitted] my pain and sorrow remain unchanged.
The fragrance of dogwood drifts down...[two words missing]...lavender;
And a breath of chrysanthemums floats in courtyard gates,
Where evening mist enshrouds the fine rain.

XXXVI. To "P'o Chen-tzu"

sɨ-	žhip	nien	lai	kya	kuk	
sam	ts'ien	li:	dhi-	šan	xhâ	
vhung-	kak	lüong	lêu	lien	siau	xan-
ngüok	žhüê-	ghyüng	tši	tsak	.yien	lâ
ki:	dzhêng	šik	kan	kuâ		

.yit	tan-	küi	üi	žhin	luê:	
šim:	.yiau	p'uan	pyin-	siau	muâ	
tsuai-	žhi-	ts'ang	xhuang	zhɨ	miau-	rit
kyau-	fang	yiu	tsêu-	bhiat	li	kâ
žhüi	lüi-	tuai-	kiong	ngâ		

In this House and Domain of forty years duration,
These hills and rivers three thousand leagues in breadth,
The Phoenix Hall and Dragon Pavilion were linked to the Celestial
     River,
And jade trees with jewel branches formed a tangled haze;
Never had we knowledge of the weapons of war.

One day, suddenly, we surrendered, to become but subjects and slaves;
With Shen's thin waist and P'an's streaked temples I waste away.
Hardest of all, the day I took my hurried leave of our ancestral shrine:
The court musicians went on playing the farewell songs
As I wept in front of my palace women.

Shen's thin waist: The poet and historian Shen Yüeh (441 513) once grew impatient while wait-
ing for appointment to a post for which he felt himself suited and wrote to his good friend Hsü
Mien to explain how he felt and complain of an illness that was afflicting him, "During the past
few months and weeks, I have had to take my leather belt in another notch repeatedly; when I
grasp my arms with my hands, I reckon that they have shrunk by half an inch in a month." Hsü
brought Shen's plight to the attention of the Emperor, who then made the desired appointment
(see *Nan Shih*, 57.1412).
P'an's streaked temples: When P'an Yüeh (the "Master Sandalwood" of poem VII) had reached
the ripe age of thirty-one, he noticed that his hair was turning grey. This moved him to compose
his well-known "Rhapsody on the Inspiration of Autumn," one passage of which reads, "My
streaked temples are grey where they receive my cap; white hairs come loose and trail down
my neck" (*Wen Hsüan*, 13.6b [177]).

XXXVII. To "Lang T'ao Sha Ling"

liam	nguai-	üê:	džhan	džhan		
tš'ün	.i-	tsiang	lan			
lâ	kim	put	nuan:	nguê:	kyêng	xhan
mong-	li:	put	tri	šin	žhi-	k'yêk
.yit	šiang-	t'am	xuan			

dhok	dzhɨ-	mak	bhing	lan		
vuê	xhyan-	kwan	šan			
bhiat	žhi	yüong	yi-	kyian-	žhi	nan
liu	šüi:	lak	xwa	küi	k'iê-	yia:
t'ien	žhiang-	rin	kyan			

Outside the blinds rain drips and splashes;
The mood of spring is soon to fade.
Gossamer covers cannot ward off the chill of the last night watch;
Within my dreams I can ignore this sojourner's life of mine,
And just for a moment yearn for joy.

I should not lean alone against a railing:
Endless, the towering mountains.
So easy it seemed to take my leave, how hard to ever meet!
A flowing river, falling blossoms, gone all away;
Heaven above, and the world of men....

Supplement: Tz'u *Poems by Li Yü not Included in the* Nan-T'ang Erh-chu Tz'u

A. To "Yü-fu"

lang-	xwa	iu:	.i-	ts'ien	drhüong	süat
dhau	li:	vuê	ngien	.yit	dhuai-	tš'ün
.yit	xhuê	tsiu:				
.yit	kan	šin				
k'wai-	xhuat	riê	nong	iu:	ki:	rin

Blossoms of spray have formed on purpose a thousand layers of snow;
Flowering peaches stand in silence, a whole legion of spring.
A single jug of wine,
A single bamboo rod,
How many men can there be in the world, as contented and jolly as me?

This poem and the next come from the *Wu-tai Ming-hua Pu-yi* ("A Supplement to *Great Painters of the Five Dynasties*," p. 116) of Liu Tao-ch'un, who had seen them added in Li Yü's own calligraphy to a painting of a fisherman done by the Southern T'ang court artist Wei Hsien (Yü-fu means "fisherman"). Although Wang Kuo-wei thought the poems too ordinary in style to be Li's work (*Nan T'ang Erh-chu Tz'u Pu-yi*, p. 6749), there is no firm evidence to support a rejection of Liu Tao-ch'un's judgment. For a thorough account of the origins of the "Yü-fu" subgenre, see Murakami, "Gyofu no Shi Kô."

B. To "Yü-fu"

.yit	drhau-	tš'ün	fung	.yit	yiap	tšiu
.yit	lün	kyian:	lüê:	.yit	k'ying	kêu
xwa	muan:	tšiê:				
tsiu:	ying	.êu				
van-	k'yüng:	puâ	triong	têk	dzhɨ-	yiu

The spring breeze my only oar, a single leaf-like boat;
A strand of silk my only line, a single dainty hook....
Blossoms cover the banks,
Wine brims in my bowl,
I find my freedom out on the limitless expanse of waves.

C. To "Liu-chih"

fung	dzhing	dzhiam-	lau:	kyian-	tš'ün	siu
tau-	tš'iê-	siau	xhun	kam:	ghiu-	yiu
tâ	zhia-	drhiang	dhiau	zhɨ-	siang	šik
ghiang	žhüi	.yien	t'ai-	fut	rin	dhêu

My romantic heart—now that I am old—is ashamed when spring
    appears;
Everywhere my stricken soul is moved for companions of long ago.
How diffident I feel before these long boughs that seem to know me,
Forcing their hazy forms to trail down low and stroke my head.

This poem is sometimes classified as a *shih*, and sometimes as a *tz'u*. It is recorded in several Sung dynasty miscellanies as having been written on a fan by Li as a gift for a palace maid named Ch'ing-nu ("Lucky"). See Shao Po, *Ho-nan Shao Shih Wen-chien Hou-lu*, 17.4a and Chang Pang-chi, *Mo-chuang Man-lu*, 2.7b.

D. To "Wu Yeh T'i"

vuê	ngien	dhok	žhiang:	si	lêu
ngüat	riê	kêu			
dzhik	mak	nguê	dhong	šim	üan-
suâ:	ts'ing	ts'iu			

tsian:	put	dhuan-						
li:	xhwan	luan-						
žhi-	li	džhêu						
bhiat	žhi-	.yit	puan	tsɨ	vyi-	dzhai-	sim	dhêu

Silent and alone, I climb the western pavilion;
The moon is like a hook.
Still and forlorn, the long courtyard and its phoenix trees
Locking clear autumn in....

Scissors cannot sever it,
However unravelled, still awry;
Such is the sorrow of separation:
There is no other with such a flavour in the heart.

The earliest source for this poem, the *T'ang Sung Chu-hsien Chüeh-miao Tz'u-hsüan* of Huang
Sheng (1.15) attributes it to Li Yü, and this is probably correct, although later collections some-
times assign it to Meng Ch'ang, one of the kings of Shu.

APPENDICES

APPENDIX A

Southern T'ang *Shih* Poems

Feng Yen-ssu

I. MORNING COURT

A brass clepsydra drips at break of day;
A cock crows to the heavens by a lofty pavilion.
They force the golden locks of five portals open,
But leave the latticed blinds of three halls still hanging down.
Before the steps, the swaying green of royal willows;
Below the staves, the scattered scarlet of palace flowers.
Several rows of mandarin duck tiles in the light of dawn,
A hundred feet high, phoenix pennants in a spring breeze.
Ministers in attendance stamp and dance in double obeisance
That sagely longevity may remain forever like the southern hills.

Li Ching

I. Written on Climbing a Pavilion on the Occasion of a Heavy Snowfall on
the First Day of the Fifth Year of the *Pao-ta* Period with the Heir Pre-
sumptive Ching-sui, Prince Ching-yi of Wang, Prince Ching-k'uei of Ch'i,
the Learned Li Chien-hsün, Secretary Hsü Hsüan, and the Ch'in-cheng
Scholar Chang Yi-fang

Beaded blinds are rolled up high, there is not the slightest veil;
Everywhere we are met with the blossoms of opposite ends of the year.
Last night the breath of spring blew open the tuning pipes;
This morning a wind from the east has set the plum trees abloom.
The white forms are out to cover over the fragrant forms;
Their falling drift is much the same as the slanting drift of a dance.
Old friends and guests are at their places; wine is in the bottles,
Whose enchanting pure bouquet belongs to our house alone.

II. AN OUTING ON THE INNER LAKE
TO ENJOY THE LOTUS BLOSSOMS

Smartweed blossoms steeped in water—their blaze cannot be doused;
Water-fowl frighten the fish away—speeding silver shuttles.
As far as the eye can see, a million acres of lotus blossoms;
Scarlet and green are jumbled together, spread over the pellucid stream.
Master Sun-tzu has now beheaded the palace ladies of Wu;
There on the surface of Porcelain Pool, the heads of beautiful women....

Li Yü

I-II. MY FEELINGS (Two Poems)

I

Again I see the phoenix tree blossoms appear on ancient boughs;
A single pavilion in mist and rain, at twilight chill and drear.
Leaning on a railing with sorrow and anguish that no one comprehends,
Without my knowing, I lower my brimming tear-filled eyes.

II

The serried walls will not behold her cherished form again;
On a festive day, shrouded in anguish, I cannot keep hold of myself.
The old hazy moon of bygone years remains to no avail,
Over Lotus Blossom Pool, a weeping moth eyebrow....

III-IV. PLUM BLOSSOMS (two poems)

I

With anxious care transplanted to this site,
Along meandering fences and low balustrades.
We pledged to meet when their fragrant season returned,
Our only concern, they might not be lovely enough.
We set up screens to protect them from the wind,

Came by moonlight with water from cold springs.
Who would have thought the blossoms would come and go,
While her moth-eyebrows instead did not survive....

II

That my tender of mist and blossoms now is gone
The Lord of Spring of course is unaware;
Of what use any more this pure fragrance
That blooms again on the boughs of bygone years?

V. WRITTEN ON A NAPKIN FOR A SACRIFICIAL BANQUET

In this drifting life, suffering weary and haggard,
Her grace and beauty were lost in the bloom of youth.
Perspiring hands have left a trace of fragrance,
Pencilled eyebrows a stain of jet black haze.

VI. WRITTEN ON THE BACK OF A *P'I-PA* GUITAR

Slender and graceful, tapering away as though cut,
It can hardly bear more than a few thin strands.
A heavenly fragrance lingers on the phoenix plume,
Her last gentle warmth in the sandalwood body.

VII–VIII. POEMS OF MOURNING (Two Poems)

I

A pearl is broken, a jewel before my eyes;
A blossom withers, in a spring beyond the world.
Before the grief in my heart could melt away,
I lost another life that I held dear.
A jade jar still contains the last of her medicine;
Her fragrant powder-case is already smudged with dust.
My initial grief is joined by a later ache—
I have no more tears to dampen my mourning cloth.

II

Her beautiful substance was like the fragrant trees,
Drifting, helpless, really much the same.
Just as I grieve for the fruit that falls in spring,
I suffer too for a thicket pounded by rains.
Where is that rich and verdant beauty now?
Blown all away, a life already nothing.
Sinking, sinking, nowhere to be sought,
Leave of the east wind taken for a thousand years.

IX. POEM OF MOURNING

Eternal memories hard to loosen or dispel;
Orphan longing—I sigh to myself in pain.
Rains deepen autumn's lonely desolation;
Sorrow draws with it illness ever graver.
Sobs choke off my thoughts before the wind;
Twilight dims my failing, beclouded sight.
The King of Emptiness should take thought for me,
My child bereft, and now gone astray from home.

X. WRITTEN AT THE END OF THE *CHIN-LOU-TZU*

According to Emperor Yuan of Liang, "Long ago, Wang Ts'an wrote many poems at Ching-chou, but when that place was ruined, he burned all of his writings. Now only a single piece survives. It is highly valued by all well-known scholars, but 'to see one hair of a tiger is not to know of its stripes!'" Later, the Western Wei captured Chiang-ling, and the Emperor also burned all of his writings, saying, "The Way of Emperors Wen and Wu is extinguished tonight!" How is it that Ching-chou was ruined and the writings burnt, the sequence being the same in both accounts? I have composed a poem of lament for this.

Ivory labelled, ten thousand scrolls, wrapped in scarlet silk....
The writings of Wang Ts'an were all consigned to burn in the fire.
Were it not that the First Emperor retains his name in the world,
How could these remnant chapters have come down to the present day?

XI. FEELINGS WHILE ILL

In this past year my weary grief has deepened;
My lonely desolation aches all the more.
The might of the wind invades my ailing bones;
The gloom of the rain strangles my sorrowing heart.
By night the tripods are used for brewing herbs;
In the morning half my beard is tinged with frost.
What could I have done in some former existence?
Who will ask this of the King of Emptiness for me?

XII. WRITTEN WHILE ILL

In ailing health or strong and well, my love for the Way is deep;
Sitting in meditation in a pure fragrance, my thoughts become
    composed.
The moon that shines on my quiet home is only a "medicine grinder";
The bars to the gates of my secluded compound are nothing but "luring
    birds."
I am loath to listen to worthless doctors; their prescriptions are no use!
The strength of the little maid who helps me walk is not sufficient.
I must enquire at the Empty Gate to know fragrance and taste,
For otherwise I torment my thoughts, and a myriad stains encroach.

XIII. JOTTED DOWN ON THE TENTH DAY OF THE NINTH MONTH

To evening rain, the gloom of autumn, from wine abruptly sobered—
Moved by the season, the strands of my heart are loose and hard to
    subdue.
Yellow blossoms wither and fall, their ripeness unattained;
Reddened leaves rustle and murmur, the rolling of distant drums.
Rejecting the world, I am truly able to weary of vulgar poses;
Accepting my fate, I still have not forgotten all my feelings.
And now that both my glossy temples are stained with streaks of white,
Though I never thought I was P'an An-jen, I still am quite surprised.

XIV. AUTUMN WARBLER

Why does the last warbler not care that autumn comes?
Flying low past the still woods it wanders still alone.
To its endless varied calls I incline my ear and listen;
A single speck of deep brown, it glides into the mist.
Resting at ease or abandoning the world, it grieves for Lu all the same;
Pure and bright, a sound like piping shattered in its throat.
Remain no longer lingering here, best to go back home;
The dew-wet flowers are chill and damp, the smart-weed blossoms sad.

XV. GETTING UP WHILE ILL: WRITTEN UPON THE WALL OF MY MOUNTAIN LODGE

Now that this mountain lodge is finished, my illness suddenly relents;
Thornwood staff and rough clothing suit my idle spirits.
The stove is open to a low fire with deep reflected warmth;
A channel leads a new stream through several murmuring meanders.
Briefly I agree with P'eng and Chüan to settle my rotten substance,
But meet in the end with Tsung and Yuan to ask about birthlessness.
How can I simply fuss and toil, tied up in this dusty world,
Anxious to contend with fish and dragons to make a mighty name?

XVI. ON SAYING FAREWELL TO MY YOUNGER BROTHER TS'UNG-YI, THE PRINCE OF TÊNG, WHO IS GOING AWAY TO GOVERN HSÜAN-CH'ENG

Preface

The autumn hills are bright and lustrous, the autumn rivers pellucid and empty. Setting your sail, you are swiftly on your way, "not regarding a thousand leagues as distant." Now that you are leaving on your mission, how troubled I am! To cultivate virtue that is everlasting is the spacious order of Heaven; to establish words that will be imperishable is the constant Way of the gentleman. Now, on account of the status of your father and elder brother, you enjoy a wealth of bells and tripods. Damsels from Wu and jewels from Chao are not what great men treasure; how much less should you, having them all! Mournful tears and sweet words are truly the constant refrain of women, and thus not what I would choose to express. As we approach the parting of the way, are these words and nothing more? Hearts set by "on the plain," this is where they will appear! Ah! The common people are neither disorderly nor obedient; love them and they will return your devotion. The petty officials are neither pure nor corrupt; exert your good influence on them and they will respond in kind. Dispensing justice is the basis of government; you must attend to it exhaustingly and lovingly. The people are central to government; you must not fail to be pure and upright. Hold to absolute justice in directing your subordinates, and flatterers and sycophants will get rid of themselves; investigate the innate natures of the fragrant and the rank, and you will never confuse beauty with ugliness. Practice the arts of war only in due season, being careful not to cause difficulty or damage to the five elements. Study and improve yourself, do not give up on this even in your free time. Do not drink to the point of losing your self-control; neither rejoice to the extent of being unruly in spirit. If you hearken conscientiously to these words you should have little occasion for regret. If you have put them into practice and wish to improve still more, the illustrious policies of the former kings are all to be found in their azure cases. Alas! Even when your elder brother was in his best years and healthy of mind he could not make his words into literature; now in his twilight years and weary at heart, how much less can his words match his thoughts! Just now we are in the cool of autumn, the eighth month. As your keel hums along the great River, I envy you this voyage. Enjoy its lofty inspiration to the full! Especially the hills and glens of Ching-t'ing, stretching into the distant vistas, for this is just the season for them!

> But keep your light skiff moored and linger just a while,
> As we pour again the wine of separation, sorry to be parting hands.
> The vast waves compel our sorrow with light that gleams and glitters;
> Jagged mountains congeal our heartache with colours high and low.
> You hasten away by juniper oar; our sadness has no end;
> I lean against a balustrade as the sun turns toward the west.
> How many lands lie along this stretch of misty river!
> No need to cherish any more the chill sadness in your heart.

XVII. GAZING AT STONE WALL FROM MIDRIVER AND WEEPING

> South of the River, north of the River, our former native land;
> For thirty years past, no more than the scene of a single dream.
> The palaces and chambers of the Garden of Wu are now cold and
>   forlorn;
> The terraces and halls of Kuang-ling town already chill and overgrown.
> Clouds veil the distant crags, a thousand dabs of sorrow;
> Raindrops drum on our surrender boat in uncounted streams of tears.
> We brothers, four of us—some three hundred men....
> I cannot bear to sit here idle, brooding on every detail.

Li Yü: Prose Writings

I. DIRGE FOR CHAO-HUI, THE EMPRESS CHOU

Heaven is constant and earth eternal,
    but halting and hindered the lot of mankind!
No sooner are craving and desire overcome,
    than grief and suffering grow tangled and wild.
Attachments and emotions reside for long terms;
    things that affect us come to the crossing.
Riches build up and life is easy,
    then happiness fades and sorrow waxes.
The sinking crow and precipitous hare,
    make summer flourish and springtime wither.
The years stretch out as my thoughts roam widely;
    I call up the bygone and forget the recent.
Past ruined vistas and crumbling shores,
    the years go by like a river's flow.
The emotions conveyed by external things
    even wounded the men of old....

(Foolishly dreaming of Kao-t'ang Terrace,
    vainly boasting of the Cove on the Lo;
They built on the void of Ch'ü Yuan,
    a source of anguish to the end of time.)

How much more so the urgings of my heart,
    whose welling grief has a real source!
Heaven above! what was our fault?
    you have destroyed my mate and companion.
Modest and retiring, difficult of access,
    she was not fated to stay in this world.
Lustrous as nephrite, glowing like a pearl,
    now she has perished, broken and crushed.

Her gentle manner and distinguished nature
    were uniquely radiant and rarely matched.
Slender but hearty, a perfect blossom,
    her gentle youthfulness bloomed and increased.
Well-formed, but not to the point of plumpness,
    sharp of wit, but never hurtful.

She needed no reminders on bowl or sash,
    caution and gravity were her only rules.
In rings and pendants she showed restraint,
    maintaining her standards at every moment.
Whether frowning or happily smiling,
    her preeminent excellence had a superior fragrance.
Her cloud-like temples retained a gleam,
    the sparkle in her eyes danced and glimmered.
The surge of her emotions had the charm of springtime,
    her words of love were a fragrance on the wind.
Her elegant carriage was heaven-sent,
    gold refined for a precious omen.
Her compliant manner gave no offence,
    and served as a model on every side.
Far far away, she has vanished alone;
    in what region has she abandoned me?

Long ago, when we were "newly married,"
    "I feasted you," and our hearts were full.
The go-between did not struggle with her speeches,
    nor had the diviners to distort the signs.
The "Return of the Maid" forecast completion,
    the trigram "All" accorded with the auguries.
"Looking up and down," "our hearts united,"
    "bound together," "in this way."
"I took you by the hand,
    that we might grow old together."
But now what has befallen us,
    that we have not fulfilled those early predictions?
Alas, alas!

Her heart and mind were fully perfected,
    her love and obedience wholly complete.
Earnest and serious her gentle grasp,
    with strength to turn harsh words away.
The love she has left is vast and deep;
    my grieving tears flow unceasingly down.
Who could have so hard a heart,
    to read this record of my grief?

Surpassing beauty readily withers;
    a "string of cities" is easily broken.

In fact, her abilities and appearance
    could intoxicate the strongest mind.
Truly, if such beauty could be eaten,
    it would satisfy one's morning hunger.
How is it that so suddenly,
    our shared hearts were in different worlds?
Alas, alas!

Such abundant talents and manifold skills,
    such a woman, fit to be followed!
In all sorts of games she showed her skill;
    seated at chess she excelled above all.
Her charm enlivened our drinking matches,
    her songs were entwined in gentle accord.

With hand-held timbrels she was in her element;
    on uncommon instruments she brought out beauty.
A halcyon dragon once upraised,
    her scarlet sleeves were flying blossoms.
Her emotions raced to the bounds of heaven;
    her thoughts came to rest on cloudy banks.
Mounting aloft or held in check,
    gently restrained or broadly expansive,
She was unique and entirely perfect,
    never showing the slightest flaw.
Those wise in harmony halted in admiration;
    those accomplished in music sighed in ecstasy.

Of songs, she performed the "Approaching Slowly,"
    of prestos, transmitted the "Urge to Dancing."
Briskly plucking with flying hands,
    her supertonic resounded and her dominant challenged.
In measure she altered the usual metres;
    in mode she changed the traditional rules.
She trimmed and removed all busy gestures,
    made a new standard strong and complete.

The ancient "Song of Rainbow Skirts,"
    its hidden tones were lost to the world.
The flavour effacing music of Ch'i
    could even afflict Confucius himself.
Those remnant sounds of the old realm,

who could bear their loss and dispersal?
It was I who fathomed its beauty,
    you who brought forth all its secrets.
You adjusted the rules of the remnant score,
    made it new and properly finished.
Who was it but you that could have done this?
    truly I had a kindred spirit.
But now you have perished,
    gone forever, far far away.
Alas, alas!

How manifold your perfect beauty,
    how full and lovely your fragrant manner!
Things are passed down to distant ages,
    but people cannot go along with them.
I gaze upward into the vacant halls,
    seeking a trace of you in vain.

I mourn our bygone happy days
    that my heart retains and my eyes remember.
The sun was dawning on ornate roof tiles,
    the breeze was warm on carven door plaques.
Flying swallows joined in singing,
    flowing waters linked their colours.
Butterflies churned the falling blossoms;
    the rains cleared up at Cold Food season.
We linked our carriages, utterly joyful,
    banqueting here and resting there.

"Mountain cherries offered their fruit";
    the fearsome sun glided through the void.
The woods were striped with late bamboo;
    lotuses danced in scattered scarlet.
Mist was light as a beautiful garment,
    snow glistened like a powdered face.
Slender eyebrows modeled on the moon,
    a tall chignon that moved with the breeze.
"With your countenance friendly and mild,"
    in what pleasure did it not accord?

Cicadas' trilling hummed with sorrow;
    elm trees withered and shed with sadness.

The utter grief of the four seasons,
   was gathered at our autumn banquets.
But our hearts were without concern,
   no external thing could cause disorder.
Sonorous were your *ch'ing* and *shang* notes,
   voluptuous your drunken gaze.
What then were your feelings like,
   as we sang and as we rested?

Cold increased in the Lily Tent;
   snowflakes danced by the Orchid Hall.
The beaded screens were rolled up at dusk,
   golden censers were fragrant in the evening.
Lovely you were, and "rouged with cinnabar,"
   "smooth and rounded, your clear brow."
"Long and peaceful, our nighttime drinking,"
   how can I ever forget you then?
Years came in and years went by,
   entirely happy in our idle pleasures.
But our time was not fulfilled,
   and former longings turned to grief.
How has it happened, so abruptly,
   is it already so long ago?
Alas, alas!

Who is it says, of those departed,
   they grow more remote as time goes by?
I long for her, that beautiful lady,
   eternally remembering, just as at first.
"I love her but I cannot see her";
   my heart seems to blaze and burn.
With chills and fever I am afflicted,
   can I ever overcome this?
Alas, alas!

The myriad things are without a heart,
   wind and mist are just as before.
There is the sun and there the moon,
   bringing shadow, bringing rain.
Inanimate things go on the same,
   but what is the lot of human beings?
Forlorn and downcast, the latticed windows,

who could bear to stay in this place?
Alas, alas!

Her beautiful name will abide forever,
    I gaze at the moon and grieve for the goddess.
Her eyes are now forever closed;
    their ripples appear no more in her mirror.
Distressed and grieving, she is lost to view;
    how will my heart endure it?

Grass and trees are chill and sad;
    grief oppresses me without limit.
One after another our former joys,
    more and more they are completely lost.

The sound of strings and pipes is stilled,
    the fragrance of silk and gossamer remote.

My thoughts well up in painful heart-ache;
    unmindful they pass beyond sorrow and anguish.
Alas, alas!

"The year is drawing to an end,"
    no date is set for us to meet.
My feelings are troubled and confused;
    whom can I follow and rely on now?
In times gone by, the season
    was just the same as this.
But now, it is my heart
    that is no longer the same.
Alas, alas!

The inhumanity of the spirits,
    "heaping up resentment as inward power."
No sooner had they taken my son,
    than they destroyed my wife as well.
In what year will the mirror be round again?
    on what day will the orchid's scent return?
Alas, alas!

Heaven is broad and vast;
    clouds of sorrow obscure it.

The void is dim and dark;
a mist of sorrow arises.
Your moth eyebrows are still and remote,
immured in the "beautiful city."
Your grieving chamber has a sorrowful aura,
utterly bereft of you.
Alas, alas!

The sun and moon have set the season,
tortoise and milfoil have now concurred.
Flutes and oboes mournfully sob;
the banners are held up high aloft.
Once your dragon bier is drawn away,
never will it turn back again.
Your golden chambers, a thousand autumns,
forever without a mistress.
Alas, alas!

The trees entwine their branches,
atremble and rustling in the wind.
Birds call to one another;
soaring and swooping they fly.
A mourning orphaned shadow,
who will grieve for me?
Sorrowing by myself,
agony without end!
Alas, alas!

At night awake with all my yearnings,
what sound is not a source of grief?
Everywhere I seek, but do not find;
how my heart is driven and destroyed!
Silently I cry out;
how can this go on?
Your spirit eternally departed,
we are sundered forever!
Alas, alas!

Utterly vanished, your fragrant soul,
vast and trackless your heavenly wanderings.
Stanching bloody tears, I caress your coffin,
where to ever greet you again?

If only the cloudy roads can be followed to their end,
    I hope to hear from you through magicians.
Alas, alas!

II. RHAPSODY ON REFUSING TO ASCEND THE HEIGHTS

Jade tankards of transparent wine,
    golden platters of decorated cakes,
The scent of dogwood pods is ardent,
    bold, the fragrance of chrysanthemum buds.

      Those in attendance approached and said,

It is now the peak of a beautiful season;
    you ought to visit the country and climb the heights.
Does the Imperial Garden not await your visit?
    the beauty of autumn look for your praise?

    I replied,

My strength in former days was such
    that my heart was happy and my joy unrestrained,
    as I played and relaxed with no thought of trouble.
I occupied my mind with the study of epigraphy,
    beguiled moon and flowers in composing poems.
I made light of gathering companions at Wu-ling,
    held the selection of deputies for San-Ch'in in contempt.
Measuring out pearls, I called on courtesans,
    with a braided cable, I moored my boat.
I covered walls and ceilings and thus wasted my wealth,
    discussed a myriad things and then threw away the dregs.
Little did I care that by wasting long nights in extravagance
    I was ensnaring great virtue with dissipation.
Now our stricken House is beset as though by fire,
    entwined in the disorder of tangled strands.

"I climb this ridge," and stand on tiptoe;
    "I await your return to the barrier," my eyes staring.

"There are wagtails on the plain," flying together;
I sigh for my younger brother, who has not returned.

The sky is vast and boundless, the wind, keen and chill;
My heart is ill at ease, my tears stream down.
There is no pleasure fit to be enjoyed,
    but a myriad strands of sadness entwined about me.
Alas, alas! what you propose is in no wise acceptable!

NOTES

Feng Yen-ssu

I. This poem, the only surviving *shih* by Feng Yen-ssu, is a descriptive work in the old courtly style, distinguished only by its uncommon metre—six syllables to the line rather than the usual five or seven. The daily audience held early in the morning was the central activity of the court, and was thus a well-established occasion for poems such as this one.

Li Ching

I. This poem is preserved, along with others written on the same occasion, in the *Chiang-piao Chih* ("An Account of the South"), an early historical work by Cheng Wen-pao (B.5a). This poem too is in the old courtly style, which concentrated on highly mannered descriptive poems composed on social occasions. The account of this snowfall party by Ch'en P'eng-nien, who gives the wrong date for it ("seventh year" (949) would be correct), is important for the study of Chinese painting, since it provides the only tenth-century reference to the painter Tung Yuan, later elevated to be the patriarch of the "Southern" School. Ching-yi and Ching-k'uei were younger brothers of Li Ching. Chang Yi-fang was an elderly official who eventually died of elixir poisoning.

II. Sun-tzu, the at least semi-legendary military strategist to whom the *Art of War* is attributed, was told by the King of Wu to train his palace consorts in military drill. Sun-tzu appointed two of the king's favourite women to be officers, explained the movements, and then ordered the women to perform them. When they collapsed with laughter, Sun-tzu ordered the two "officers" beheaded, to the horror of the king, after which order was restored and the survivors carried out the prescribed drill very smartly.

Li Yü

I. This poem and the six that follow are cited in the biography of Chao-hui in Ma Ling's *Nan-T'ang Shu* (6.7a–8a).

IV. The Lord of Spring is the East Wind; see the introduction for the associations involved.

VII. This poem and the two that follow were originally included in Ma Ling's biography of Chung-hsüan, Li Yü's son who died in infancy.

IX. King of Emptiness: Buddha.

X. This poem and its preface were added as a colophon to a copy of the *Chin-lou-tzu* ("Master Golden Pavilion"), a philosophical work by Hsiao Yi. Hsiao, who reigned briefly (552–54) as Emperor Hsiao-yuan of the Liang dynasty, was put to death in his capital at Chiang-ling by invaders from the north. He was a prolific writer and scholar, but burned the Imperial Library as his capital was falling. The *Chin-lou-tzu* itself was later lost, and current editions have been reconstructed on the basis of quotations in encyclopedias and other works, but we know that it was still in existence around the year 1200 because Li Yü's colophon was copied at that time into a book of miscellaneous notes by Yuan Chiung and Yuan Yi, the *Feng-ch'uang Hsiao-tu* (A.16ab). It is from this book that the poem is translated here. Since Li Yü is said to have attempted to burn his own library before his surrender, the colophon would have had a triple irony for a Sung reader. Wang Ts'an (177–217) was one of the great poets at the very end of the Han dynasty. He fled south to Chiang-ling (also known as Ching-chou) to escape the anarchy prevailing in the north. The First Emperor of Ch'in is famous for his book-burning campaign, one of whose results was ironically the heightened awareness among the Chinese of the importance of preserving written documents.

XI. This poem and the one following were preserved in Fang Hui's anthology *Ying-k'uei Lü-sui* (c.1300), with a note saying that Li Yü's collected works contained many poems inspired by illness (44.5a, 9b). For the "King of Emptiness," see above.

XII. The second couplet of this poem makes use of a kind of double parallelism that is not infrequently found in regulated verse. The last two words in each line are literally "grind herbs" and "attract birds," which are parallel in their corresponding parts. But "grinding herbs" refers to the legendary hare who lives in the moon, where he grinds the elixir of immortality. And "attract birds" is a name for the apple trees that apparently grew in Li's courtyard. The "Empty Gate" is Buddhism.

XIII. P'an An-jen is P'an Yüeh, see Li's *tz'u* XXXVI. This poem and the three that follow are no longer found in any source earlier than the Ch'ing dynasty (1644–1911), although it is likely that they were copied from now lost works of the Sung period.

XIV. Lu is the old name for what is now part of Honan province. It lies several hundred miles to the north of Nanking. I have devoted many days to a search for a classical allusion behind this line, but have found none, so perhaps it simply means what it says, that the bird is lingering in its seasonal migration because of homesickness for its home in the north.

XV. P'eng Tsu and Chüan Tzu were legendary Methuselahs associated in Chinese tradition with Taoist arts of longevity. Lei Tz'u-tsung and Hui-yuan were early Buddhist leaders.

XVI. This poem and the long preface that accompanies it were written in 968. The phrase about regarding a thousand leagues as distant comes from the opening of the *Mencius*; that mentioning "on the plain" from the *Songs*, where the line "wagtails on the plain" refers to the love between brothers.

XVII. The authenticity of this poem is very doubtful, since the relative abundance of internal and external evidence provided by early sources is open to various interpretations. I tend to agree with Hsia Ch'eng-t'ao and Kung Ying-tê (rather than with Yu Kuo-en, in the *T'ao-lun Chi*, p. 72) that the poem is by Yang P'u, the last of Yang Hsing-mi's sons, who is supposed to have written it after he was deposed by "Li Pien." An additional poem attributed to Li Yü in Li O's *Sung Shih Chi-shih* (86.4a) is definitely spurious. The author's name, Li Fu-kuei, is given correctly elsewhere in the same work (26.15a), as well as in its source, the *Wu-chün Chih* of Fan Ch'eng-ta (32.5a).

Prose Works of Li Yü

Li Yü's surviving prose writings are extremely miscellaneous in character. Moreover, some of them are extant only in abridged or even paraphrased versions. Only three pieces are of any interest as literary works: the preface to poem XVI, and the dirge and "refusal" given here. Although neither would ever be classified as poetry in the Chinese tradition, both are rhymed— I have represented the changes in rhyme as stanza breaks in translation—and both show some degree of metrical regularity. The dirge, in particular, is in a regular four-word metre until its closing lines.

I. If Li Yü's dirge for Chao-hui seems original, or unlike anything the reader has encountered before in Chinese literature, this is, alas, only because no one has, to my knowledge, bothered to render a real "dirge" (*lei*) into English hitherto. The form was very old by the time Li Yü turned his hand to this one, and its conventions were well established. The solemnity of the occasion demanded that language of the greatest seriousness and antiquity be used. As a result, some passages of the dirge are little more than patchworks made up of two, four, and eight word bits from old texts, chiefly the *Changes* and the *Songs*. In many cases these add nothing to the meaning of the text beyond a measure of dignity, and it would be tedious to list their sources one by one. Most of those that I know to be drawn from old texts I have put in quotation marks, but only those that seem likely to require explanation are commented on here. The crow and hare refer to the sun and moon respectively. The poetic style created by Ch'ü Yuan (third century B.C., author of the "Li Sao," "Nine Songs," and a few other poems included in the anthology *Ch'u Tz'u*—"Songs of the South") was developed into the Han rhapsody (*fu*). Two important works in this latter form, both written on romantic themes, were Sung Yü's "Rhapsody on Kao-t'ang" (source of the story about the goddess of "clouds and rain," see introduction. For a discussion of the original rhapsody and an annotated translation, see Lois Fusek, "The Kao-t'ang Fu") and Ts'ao Chih's "The Goddess of the River Lo." Chao-hui's biography records that she composed pieces of music called "Approaching Slowly"—probably an allusion to the drinking rule that the guest to whom the wine was served last was to drink three cups in quick succession, to make up for having had to wait—and the "Urge to Dancing." For her work on the "Song of Rainbow Skirts," see notes to Li Yü's *tz'u* XXVIII. When Confucius heard the court music of Ch'i, he was so moved by it that he forgot the flavour of meat for several months.

II. The occasion for the refusal announced in this piece, written in 974, was not simply pique. Li was saddened by the prolonged detention of his younger brother Ts'ung-shan at the Sung court. Wu-ling ("Five Tombs") was an area near the old capital Ch'ang-an. It was known as the home of many brave fighters. San-Ch'in ("Three Districts of Ch'in") refers to the three principalities that Hsiang Yü established in southern Shensi after he had put an end to the Ch'in dynasty. He appointed three loyal generals to rule them. Li Yü's point in this couplet is that he has neglected his duty by neither gathering brave soldiers nor selecting worthy officials. The phrases in quotation marks are from the *Songs*. For "the wagtails," see notes to *shih* poem XVI.

APPENDIX B

Tz'u Misattributed to Li Ching or Li Yü

I. TO "SAN T'AI LING"   *Anon. T'ang*

Sleepless, I weary of waiting out the long watches,
Rise and dress, go out of doors and walk.
The moon is cold, the autumn bamboo frosty;
The wind is keen, and windows rattle in the night.

II. RETURNING TO THE HILLS   *Ku K'uang*

For the concerns of my heart, a few strands of white hair;
For the limit of my life, a single slip of the blue hills....
There is snow to await me in the bare woods,
No one on the old road as I return alone.

III. TO "KENG-LOU-TZU"   *Wen T'ing-yün*

The willow floss is long,
The springtime rains are fine;
Beyond the blossoms the sound of a water-clock far away.
Alarming geese from the steppe frontier,
Arousing crows on the city walls,
On a painted screen, golden partridges....

A thin haze of incense
Seeps through blinds and curtains;
Sad and forlorn the pools and pavilions of the Hsieh.
Scarlet candles put aside,
Embroidered curtains hanging.
My dreams drag on, and yet you do not care.

IV. TO "HUAN HSI SHA" *Yen Shu*

A single newly written song, of wine a single cup,
Weather the same as in bygone years, familiar pavilions and terraces....
An evening sun descends in the west; when will it return?

There is no help, no remedy, the blossoms fade and fall;
I seem to have known some time before the swallows that return,
As to and fro I walk alone the fragrant paths of a tiny garden.

V. TO "HUAN HSI SHA" *Su Shih*

A wind presses light clouds scudding low across the river;
It clears for a moment, and swallows squabble for mud by ponds and
    halls.
Master Shen is often ill, and cannot bear to dress.

Upon the sands we have no news conveyed by migratory geese;
Partridge calls in bamboo groves are heard from time to time.
Such feelings as these are heeded by none but falling blossoms.

VI. TO "CH'ANG HSIANG SSU" *Teng Su*

One range of hills,
Two ranges of hills,
Distant the hills, high the heavens, and cold the misty rivers:
Maple leaves crimson with lovers' thoughts....

Chrysanthemums blossom,
Chrysanthemums fade,
Wild geese have flown to the west, but he has not returned;
Wind and moonlight idle in a single blind.

VII. TO "TAO LIEN-TZU" *T'ien Chung-hsing*

Cloudy tresses tousled,
Evening powder faded,
She knits a pair of sulky brows in a range of distant hills.
Her fragrant cheeks are held aslant by tender spring bamboo;
On whose account do her warm tears flow, leaning against the
   balustrade?

VIII. TO "HOU-T'ING HUA P'O-TZU" *Yuan Hao-wen*

A tree of jade before the inner garden,
Jewel flowers beside the dressing mirrors;
Last year's blossoms are not yet old,
While this year's new moon shines full again.
Do not urge bias;
Join the blossoms, join the moon,
As all together we enjoy long years of youth.

NOTES

The canon of Li Yü's genuine *tz'u* is singularly ill-defined. That one poem included in the *Nan-T'ang Erh-chu Tz'u*, Wen T'ing-yün's lyric to "Keng-lou-tzu" (cited in the Introduction), is spurious cannot be doubted, since it was included in the *Hua-chien Chi*, edited when Li Yü was three years old. But the authenticity of many of the other poems in the collection has been challenged as well. The most serious of these challenges are probably those concerning poems I and XXIV, which are also found in the *Yang-ch'un Chi*, and the second of these at least, may very well be by Feng Yen-ssu. Other poems of contested authorship are II–IV, VII, XII, XV, XVII–XVIII, XX, XXVI, XXVIII, and the last three lines of X. There are, in addition, a considerable number of other *tz'u*—Wang Chung-wen gives twenty-three—that have been attributed to either Li Ching or Li Yü in one source or another. I have added to the translation of the *Nan-T'ang Erh-chu Tz'u* itself the four among these that it seems reasonable to accept as possibly Li Yü's work. Many of the others are simply impossible attributions owing to various combinations of accident and ignorance on the part of—as the Ming critic Yang Shen remarks with dismay anent one of the more preposterous cases—"one knows not what sort of madman" (*Tz'u-p'in*, 2.11b). These two groups of poems aside, there remain ten poems that clearly are not by either father or son, but which are so often treated as if they were that it would seem an omission to neglect them entirely here. One of these is the one to "Keng-lou-tzu" by Wen T'ing-yün mentioned above. Another is Feng Yen-ssu's "Huan Hsi Sha," poem L among our selections from the *Yang-ch'un Chi*. Particulars concerning the other eight are given here, based on material gathered by Wang Chung-wen.

I. This poem was first attributed to Li Yü in a Ch'ing dynasty work. It is elsewhere said to be by the T'ang poet Wei Ying-wu, but this is probably mistaken too.

II. This poem was said to have been "written out"—that is, as an example of calligraphy—by Li Yü, and T'ang Kuei-chang, in preparing his edition of the *tz'u*, took this to mean that he had composed it as well. But it is known to be by the eighth century nature poet Ku K'uang.

III. This poem was attributed to Li Yü in the early Sung *tz'u* anthology *Tsun-ch'ien Chi*, but it is, like the other misattributed "Keng-lou-tzu" lyric, included in the *Hua-chien Chi* as Wen T'ing-yün's work, and this is certainly correct. The Hsieh family was one of the wealthiest and most prominent clans of southern China during the Six Dynasties period. Murakami Tetsumi has devoted an article, " 'Shokuhai,' 'Teihai' to iu Koto," to the meaning of the phrase "candles put aside," citing many relevant examples from a wide variety of sources.

IV. This poem and the next were included in an early anthology of *tz'u* following the first of Li Ching's poems to the same melody and without any author's name attached. From this circumstance, both were occasionally taken to be Li Ching's work as well. But in fact both are by important Northern Sung poets, being included in their collections of lyrics, which predate the misleading anthology.

V. For Shen Yüeh and his ill health, see the notes to Li Yü poem XXXVI.

VI. This poem was included in an early *tz'u* anthology as an anonymous work, and Li Yü's name was later attached to it. But it is by a Northern Sung poet, Teng Su (1091–1133), in whose collected works it is found.

VII. This poem was actually added to the *Nan-T'ang Erh-chu Tz'u* by Lü Yuan, whose edition, published during the Ming dynasty, is generally considered the earliest and best of those presently extant. But it is not found attributed to Li Yü in any source earlier than the Ming dynasty. Wang Chung-wen has recently established, by means of a very neat piece of detective work, that it must be the only surviving lyric by a now forgotten poet named T'ien Chung-hsing who, was probably active during the first half of the twelfth century.

VIII. This poem was unaccountably attributed to Li Yü in a Ming dynasty work, but it is clearly by the Chin poet Yuan Hao-wen (1190–1257).

BIBLIOGRAPHY

Abbreviations

LHTT   *Li Hou-chu ho T'a ti Tz'u* [Li Yü and His Lyric Poems]. 2 vols. Taipei: T'ai-wan Hsüeh-sheng Shu-chü, 1971.

PP   *Pai-pu Ts'ung-shu Chi-ch'eng* (references to this reprint series, preceded by the name of the original *ts'ung-shu*, are given in the form "PP a/b," in which "a" is the number of the series, and "b" the number of the case within the series).

PT   Wright, Arthur F., and Denis Twitchett, eds. *Perspectives on the T'ang*. New Haven and London: Yale University Press, 1973.

A. BASIC SOURCES

1. Editions of the Poems

There is no really adequate modern edition of the *Yang-ch'un Chi*. I have used the handy *Yang-ch'un Chi Chien* [Annotated Springtime Collection] of Cheng Yu-ch'ing 鄭郁鄉 (Chia-hsing Shui-ni Kung-ssu Wen-hua Chi-chin-hui Yen-chiu Lun-wen, no. 248. Taipei?, 1973) as my working text, checking it continually against several older editions to avoid being led astray by its not infrequent misprints. Although Cheng's textual apparatus is sometimes not all that one might wish for, his explanatory notes are often helpful, and his commentary on the poems is occasionally enlightening as well.

In the case of the *Nan-T'ang Erh-chu Tz'u*, I have used, with unfailing appreciation, the *Nan-T'ang Erh-chu Tz'u Chao-ting* [Collated and Confirmed Text of the "Lyric Poems of the Two Lords of Southern T'ang"] of Wang Chung-wen 上仲聞 (Peking: Jen-min Wen-hsüeh Ch'u-pan-she, 1957; also reprinted as Wang Tz'u-ts'ung 次聰 , "*Nan-T'ang Erh-chu Tz'u* Chiao-chu" [Collated and Annotated Text of the "Lyric Poems of the Two Lords of Southern T'ang"] in a volume entitled *Nan-T'ang Erh-chu Tz'u* [*Yang ch'un Chi*] Taipei: Shih-chieh Shu-chü, 1965), which is a model of everything that a critical edition of a Chinese literary text ought to be—and almost never is. The older *Nan-T'ang Erh-chu Tz'u Hui-chien* [Collected Annotations on the "Lyric Poems of the Two Lords of Southern T'ang"] (1936; Reprint. Taipei: Cheng-chung Shu-chü, 1971) of T'ang Kuei-chang 唐圭璋 remains useful. Chan-An-t'ai's 詹安泰 *Li Ching Li Yü Tz'u* [Lyric Poems of Li Ching and Li Yü] (Peking: Jen-min Wen-hsüeh Ch'u-pan-she, 1958; introduction reprinted, with the author's name given as Lu Ling-sheng 陸嶺生 , in LHTT, 1:13–62) has helpful explanatory notes.

2. Translations

Only a few scattered poems by Feng Yen-ssu have appeared in translation hitherto. In contrast, Li Yü has probably been translated more often, in proportion to the limited corpus of his surviving work, than any comparable Chinese poet. Neither of the two outstanding complete translations is in English. One is Alfred Hoffmann's *Die Lieder des Li Yü* (937–978): *Herrschers der Südlichen T'ang-Dynastie* (Cologne: Greven Verlag, 1950). The other is in a volume by Murakami Tetsumi 村上哲見 , *Ri Iku* [Li Yü] (Chūgoku Shijin Senshū, vol. 16. Tokyo: Iwanami Shoten, 1959). Hoffmann is hampered by his unavoidable reliance on a very inferior edition of the Chinese text, but he brings to the poems a thorough knowledge of the conventions of the *tz'u* and a profound understanding of their meaning and imagery. Murakami is a leading Japanese scholar in the field of Chinese lyric poetry, and his translation and notes are very useful. Two other standard partial Japanese translations are to be found in *Rekidai Meishisen*, [A Selection of Great Lyric Poems from Every Age] (Kanshi Taikei, vol. 24, compiled and translated by Nakata Yūjirō 中田勇次郎 . Tokyo: Shūeisha, 1965), pp. 159–76 (four poems by Feng Yen-ssu, two by Li Ching, and seven by Li Yü), and *Sōdai Shishū* [Collected Lyric Poems of the Sung Period] (Chūgoku Koten Bungaku Taikei, vol. 20, compiled by Kuraishi Takeshirō 倉石武四郎. Tokyo: Heibonsha, 1970), pp. 53–63 (two by Feng, four by Li Ching, and twenty-two by Li Yü).

Two of the three complete English translations known to me are in unpublished theses. The third is Liu Yih-ling and Shahid Suhrawardy's *Poems of Lee Hou-chu* (Bombay: Orient Longmans, 1948), mercifully long out of print. Far and away the best of the three is included in Sam Houston Brock, Jr.'s, "The Tz'u of Li Hou-chu" (Master's thesis, Columbia University, 1947), selections from which are reprinted in Cyril Birch, ed., *Anthology of Chinese Literature: From Early Times to the Fourteenth Century*, pp. 348–352 (New York: Grove Press, 1965). Stephen Shu-ning Liu's dissertation, "The Lyrics of Li Yü: A Translation, Analysis, and Commentary" (Ph.D. dissertation, University of North Dakota, 1973) also includes a complete translation, but this is undistinguished, and the thesis itself is marred by uncritical handling of its sources. It hardly seems worthwhile to list all the less than complete translations of Li Yü's poems into English that have appeared in scattered places over the years but one of them, at least, cannot be passed over in silence. This is Arthur Waley's "Immeasurable Pain," a version of our poem XIa, in *Chinese Poems*, (London: Unwin, 1961), p. 176, which is in a class by itself; it is one of Waley's most beautiful achievements, for all the liberties that he takes with the text.

3. Critical Studies

The chronological biographies of all three poets by Hsia Ch'eng-t'ao 夏承燾 are essential to any serious study of their works, "Feng Cheng-chung Nien-p'u" [Chronological Register for Feng Yen-ssu], *T'ang-Sung Tz'u-jen Nien-p'u* [Chronological Registers for T'ang and Sung Lyric Poets] (Shanghai: Chung-hua Shu-chü, 1961; also reprinted, Taipei: Ming-lun Ch'u-pan-she, 1970; 35–71); an earlier version is reprinted, with the author's name given as Hsia Ch'ü-ch'an 瞿禪 in the volume mentioned above under Wang Chung-wen's edition of the poems, separately paginated; and "Nan-T'ang Erh-chu Nien-p'u"; *T'ang-Sung Tz'u-jen Nien-p'u*; 73–168; also reprinted in an earlier version in the same volume as the preceding. An additional reprint, reset, is to be found in *LHTT*, 2:21–167, with the author's name given simply as Ch'ü-ch'an; another reprint is appended to the less critical account by Chang Ch'ung-yi 章崇義 , *Li Hou-chu Shih-tz'u Nien-p'u* [Chronological Register for Li Yü's Poems and Lyrics] (Hong Kong: Lung-men Shu-tien, 1969). There are two particularly good discussions of the style of the early *tz'u* poets. One is the long article by Yeh Chia-ying 葉嘉瑩 [Florence Chao], "Ts'ung *Jen-chien Tz'u-hua* K'an Wen, Wei, Feng, Li, Ssu-chia Tz'u ti Feng-ko" [The Styles of the Four Lyric Poets Wen (T'ing-yün), Wei (Chuang), Feng (Yen-ssu), and Li (Yü), as Seen from the "Poetic Remarks from the Human world"], Chia-ling T'an Tz'u [Chia-ling Discusses Lyric Poetry], pp. 55–143 (Ch'un Wen-hsüeh Ts'ung-shu, no. 28. Taipei, 1970). The other is Kang-i Sun Chang, *The Evolution of Chinese Tz'u Poetry: From Late T'ang to Northern Sung*, (Princeton: Princeton University Press, 1980).

Feng Yen-ssu has otherwise been comparatively little studied. The slim volume by Lin Wen-pao 林文寶 , *Feng Yen-ssu Yen-chiu* [Studies of Feng Yen-ssu] (Chia-hsin Shui-ni Kung-ssu Wen-hua Chi-chin-hui Yen-chiu Lun-wen, no. 297. Taipei?, 1976) is quite helpful, especially the excellent analysis of bias in early accounts of Feng's life and character, which goes beyond the work of Hsia Ch'eng-t'ao. Lin's discussion of Feng's poetry is of less interest but still useful. There is an enormous secondary literature on Li Yü in Chinese, inspired, in part, by his romantic image in literary history, but the great bulk of it ("Li Hou-chu's Love Life," etc.) is of the most thorough and unrelieved triviality. There are useful supplements to Hsia Ch'eng-t'ao—he does not mention them—in two early articles by Kung Ying-te 弓英德 , "Li Hou-chu Wang-kuo Shih-tz'u Pien-cheng" [Analytic Examination of Li Yü's Poems on the Fall of His State], *Li-hsüeh* 2 (1934): 91–97; and "Nan-T'ang Tsu-shih K'ao-lüeh" [A Brief Examination of the Genealogy of the Southern T'ang Royal House] *Li-hsüeh* 3 (1935): 34–37, and in a more recent one by Juan T'ing-cho 阮廷卓 , "Li Hou-chu chih Ssu" [The Death of Li Yü] *Ta-lu Tsa-chih* 14 (1957): 18–23.

In a class by itself is the *Li Yü Tz'u T'ao-lun Chi* [Collected Discussions of Li Yü's Lyric Poems] (Peking: Tso-chia Ch'u-pan-she, 1957), a collection of articles and other materials generated by an extensive debate over the value of Li's poems that took place in China in the mid 1950's. It was eventually concluded that he was too feudal—read bad and old-fashioned—to be a good model for modern Chinese writers or readers, but sanity (aided by a few well-chosen quotations from Lenin) seems to have prevailed in the end, and it was agreed that reading his poems, whose literary excellence was acknowledged, could do little real harm. Although the entire volume advances our knowledge of Li Yü hardly at all, it is an interesting example of the long Chinese tradition of pragmatic criticism in its modern guise, and it is encouraging to find that, however small the confidence implied in the good sense of the reading public, the debate itself was carried on at a fairly sophisticated level. The theoretical dilemma—how to deal with a "bad" author widely loved and admired by readers belonging to a variety of social classes—was squarely and, on the whole, honestly faced, and sound evidence and clear reasoning eventually prevailed over crude generalizations and vulgar misreading. One participant, Professor Mao Hsing, even questioned the wisdom of treating the *tz'u* as reliable autobiographical testimony, pointing out the conventional nature of much of their content. There are two useful discussions of the *T'ao-lun Chi* in Japanese, one in Murakami Tetsumi's "Ri Goshu no Shi ni Kansuru Tōron" [Discussions Concerning Li Yü's Lyric Poems] (*Chūgoku Bungaku Hō* 7 [1957]: 150–75), and the other in an article by Kunichi Minoru 國枝稔 , "Ri Iku no Shōgai to Sono Bungaku" [The Life and Writings of Li Yü] (*Gifu Daigaku Kenkyū Hōkoku* [*Jimbun Kagaku*] Vol. 8, no. 2 [1959]: 11–23).

Another collection of secondary articles is the two-volume set *Li Hou-chu ho T'ai ti Tz'u*, published in Taiwan (see above under "abbreviations," *LHTT*). Although far from worthless, this work must be used with some care, as the attributions of some of its contents are highly misleading. I have recorded in connection with individual items the instances that I have noticed (and similar ones with other reprints), but without feeling confident that I have entirely plumbed the depths of the publisher's disingenuousness. *Caveat lector!*

B. WORKS CITED IN TEXT AND NOTES

Aoyama Hiroshi 青山宏 . *Kakanshū Sakuin* [A Concordance to the "Among the Flowers Collection"], Tōyōgaku Bunsen Sentā Sōkan, no. 21. Tokyo: Tōkyō Daigaku Tōyō Bunka Kenkyūjō, 1974.

————. "Tō-Sō Shi ni Okeru 'Mukai' no Go ni Tsuite: Ri Iku no 'Kisen'o' Shi o Megutte" [On the Expression "Return in Dreams" in T'ang and Sung Lyric Poems, With Particular Reference to Li Yü's Lyric "Hsi Ch'ien Ying"]. *Nihon Daigaku Sakuraoka Kōtō Gakkō Kenkyū Kiyō* 1 (1967): 21–32.

Barnhart, Richard. *Marriage of the Lord of the River: a Lost Landscape by Tung Yuan,* Artibus Asiae, Supplementum XXVII. Ascona, 1970.

Baxter, Glen William. "Metrical Origins of the *Tz'u.*" *HJAS* 18 (1955): 124–41. Reprinted in *Studies in Chinese Literature,* Harvard-Yenching Institute Series 21, ed. John L. Bishop, pp. 186–224. Cambridge: Harvard University Press, 1966.

Bryant, Daniel. "The 'Hsieh Hsin En' Fragments by Li Yü and his Lyric to the Melody 'Lin Chiang Hsien.'" In Ronald Miao, ed., *Studies in Chinese Poetry and Poetics,* vol. 2. San Francisco: Chinese Materials Centre, forthcoming.

————. "Textual Notes on Some of the Sources for Southern T'ang *Tz'u* Poetry" (MS in preparation).

————. "The Landscape Painters Tung Yuan and Chü-jan in Sung Dynasty Literature" (completed MS).

————. "The Rhyming Categories of Tenth Century Chinese Poetry." *Monumenta Serica,* in press.

Chan, Marie. "The Frontier Poems of Ts'en Shen." *JAOS* 98 (1978): 420–37.

Chang Pang-chi 張邦基 . *Mo-chuang Man-lu* [Leisurely Records from Ink Manor]. *Pai-hai,* case 4; Reprint. *PP* 14/3.

Ch'ao Tsai-chih 晁載之 . *Hsü T'an-chu* [Aids to Conversation, Continued]. *Shih-wan Chüan Lou Ts'ung-shu,* third series; Reprint. *PP* 76/11.

Chen Shih-chuan. "Dates of Some of the Tunhuang Lyrics." *JAOS* 88 (1968): 261–70.

————. "The Rise of the Tz'u, Reconsidered." *JAOS* 90 (1970): 232–42.

Ch'en Chen-sun 陳振孫 . *Chih-chai Shu-lu Chieh-t'i* [Annotated Listing of Writings in the Straight Studio]. *Wu-ying Tien Chü-chen-pan Shu;* Reprint. *PP* 27/35.

Ch'en Hu 陳鵠 . *Ch'i-chiu Hsü-wen* [Things Heard from Old-timers, Continued]. *Chih-pu-tsu Chai Ts'ung-shu,* nineteenth series; Reprint. *PP* 29/18.

Ch'en T'ing-cho 陳廷焯 . *Pai-yü Chai Tz'u-hua* [Comments on Lyric Poetry from the White Rain Studio]. *Tz'u-hua Ts'ung-pien*; Reprint. Taipei: Kuang-wen Shu-chü, 1970.

Cheng Ch'ien 鄭騫 "Lun Feng Yen-ssu Tz'u" [Discussing the Lyric Poems of Feng Yen-ssu], *Ching-wu Ts'ung-pien, Shang-chi, Ts'ung Tz'u tao Ch'ü* [Collected Works of Ching-wu, First Collection, From Lyric Poems to Arias], pp. 110–12. Taipei: T'ai-wan Chung-hua Shu-chü, 1972 (originally published 1946).

Cheng Wen-pao 鄭文寶 . *Chiang-piao Chih* [An Account of the South]. *Hsüeh-hai Lei-pien*; Reprint. *PP* 24/4.

Chiang Li-tsai 蔣勵材 . *Li Hou-chu Tz'u-chuan* [A Biography (based on the) Lyric Poems of Li Yü]. Taipei: Chung-hua Ts'ung-shu Pien-shu Wei-yuan-hui, 1962. (Basic text in *Li Hou-chu Tz'u-hua* [Lyric Story of Li Yü], Hong Kong: Kuang-hua Shu-tien, 1960, and as "Tz'u-wang Li Hou-chu" [The Lyric Poet King Li Yü], issued serially in *Ch'ang-Liu*, vol. 8, no. 3 [1953], pp. 5ff.; and *Min-chu Hsien-cheng*, vol. 9, no. 11 [1956], pp. 17ff.; vol. 10, no. 1, pp. 31ff.; no. 2, pp. 17ff.; no. 3, pp. 18ff.; no. 4, pp. 19ff.; no. 5, pp. 18ff.; no. 6, pp. 20ff.; no. 7, pp. 19ff.).

Chou Mi 周密 . *Hao-jan Chai Ya-t'an* [Refined Remarks from the Vast and Overflowing (Spirit) Studio]. *Wu-ying Tien Chü-chen-pan Shu*; Reprint. *PP* 27/84.

Chou Tsu-chuan 周祖譔 . *Sui T'ang Wu-tai Wen-hsüeh Shih* [A History of Sui, T'ang, and Five Dynasties Literature]. Foochow: Fu-chien Jen-min Ch'u-pan-she, 1958.

Ch'üan T'ang Shih [Complete T'ang Poems]. Reprint. Taipei: Fu-hsing Shu-chü, 1961.

Davis, A. R., ed. *The Penguin Book of Chinese Verse*. Harmondsworth: Penguin Books, 1962.

Fan Ch'eng-ta 范成大 . *Wu-chün Chih* [An Account of the District of Wu]. *Shou-shan Ko Ts'ung-shu*; Reprint. *PP* 52/5.

Fang Hui 方回 . *Ying-k'uei Lü-sui K'an-wu* [A Corrected Edition of the "Essence of Regulated Verse from the (Mystic Isle of) Ying and K'uei (the Constellation that Governs Letters)"]. n.p., 1880.

Frankel, Hans. "T'ang Literati: A Composite Biography." In *Confucian Personalities*, ed. Arthur F. Wright and Denis Twitchett, pp. 65–83, 334–36. Stanford: Stanford University Press, 1962.

Fukumoto Masakazu 福本雅一 . "Keisokuen no Kui ni Tsuite: Takeuchi Setsu e no Gimon" [On the Meaning of "far away Chi-sai"—a Doubt Concerning Takeuchi's Explanation]. *Tezukayama Gakuin Tanki Daigaku Kenkyū Nempō* 18 (1970): 88–93.

Fusek, Lois. "The 'Kao-t'ang Fu' 高唐賦 ." *Monumenta Serica* 30 (1972–73): 392–425.

Gernet, Jacques. *Le Monde Chinois*. Paris: Librarie Armand Colin, 1972.

Giles, Herbert A. *Gems of Chinese Literature*. 2 vols. 1923; Reprint. New York: Paragon Book Reprint and Dover Publishing, 1965.

Goodrich, L. Carrington, and Chaoying Fang, eds. *Dictionary of Ming Biography 1368-1644*. New York: Columbia University Press, 1976.

van Gulik, Robert H. *Sexual Life in Ancient China: A Preliminary Survey of Chinese Sex and Society from ca. 1500 B.C. till 1644 A.D.* Leiden: E. J. Brill, 1961.

Hsi Tso-ch'ih 習鑿齒 . *Hsiang-yang Ch'i-chiu Chi* [Records of the Old-timers of Hsiang-yang]. *Hsin Chai Shih-chung*.

Hsia Ch'eng-t'ao. "Chou Ts'ao-ch'uang Nien-p'u" [A Chronological Register for Chou Mi]. *T'ang-Sung Tz'u-jen Nien-p'u*, see above, section A.3.

Hsieh Shih-ya 謝世涯 . "Lun Nan-T'ang Chung-chu Li Ching Tz'u" [On the Lyric Poems of Li Ching]. *Nan-yang Ta-hsüeh Yen-chiu-yuan, Jen-wen yü She-hui K'o-hsüeh Yen-chiu-so Yen-chiu Lun-wen* 41 (1976): 1-9.

Hsüan-ho Shu-p'u [Catalogue of Calligraphy in the Hsüan-ho (Emperor's) Collection]. *Hsüeh-chin T'ao-yuan*, eleventh series; Reprint. *PP* 46/16.

Huang Sheng 黄昇 . *T'ang-Sung Chu-hsien Chüeh-miao Tz'u-hsüan* [Selected Lyric Poems of Paramount Excellence by the Wise Men of T'ang and Sung]. Reprint. *Ssu-pu Ts'ung-k'an*.

Jen Erh-pei 任二北 *Tun-huang Ch'ü Chiao-lu* [Collated Record of the Tun-huang Songs]. Shanghai: Wen-yi Lien-ho Ch'un-pan-she, 1955.

———. *Tun-huang Ch'ü Ch'u-t'an* [Preliminary Investigation of the Tun-huang Songs]. Shanghai: Wen-yi Lien-ho Ch'u-pan-she, 1954.

Kuo Te-hao 郭德浩 . "Li Hou-chu P'ing-chuan" [A Critical Biography of Li Yü]. *LHTT*, 1:63-163.

Lai Wood-yan 黎活仁 . "Li Yü Chi-chung 'Juan Lang Kuei' yü 'Yü Mei-jen' Liang-shou Tz'u Yi-tien Hsiao Wen-t'i ti T'ao-lun" [A Discussion of a Small Problem in the Two Lyric Poems to "Juan Lang Kuei" and "Yü Mei-jen" in Li Yü's Collected Works]. *Ch'ung-chi Hsiao-k'an* 59 (1975): 33-38.

Levy, Howard S. *Biography of Huang Ch'ao*, Institute of East Asiatic Studies, University of California, Chinese Dynastic Histories Translations, no. 5. Berkeley and Los Angeles: University of California Press, 1955.

———. *Chinese Footbinding: The History of a Curious Erotic Custom*. New York: Walton Rawls, 1966.

Li O 厲鶚 . *Sung Shih Chi-shih* [A Record of Events in Sung Poetry]. Reprint. Taipei: Ting-wen Shu-chü, 1971.

Liang Seng-pao 梁僧寶 . *Ssu-sheng Yün-p'u* [Rhyme Table (Arranged According to the) Four Tones]. Reprint. Taipei: Kuang-wen Shu-chü, 1967.

Lin Jui-han 林瑞翰 . "Nan-T'ang chih Ching-chi yü Wen-hua" [The Economy and Culture of Southern T'ang]. *Ta-lu Tsa-chih* 26 (1964): 183–90.

Lin, Shuen-fu. *The Transformation of the Chinese Lyrical Tradition: Chiang K'uei and Southern Sung Tz'u Poetry.* Princeton: Princeton University Press, 1978.

Liu Hsiang 劉向 . *Lieh-hsien Chuan* [Biographies of the Transcendants]. *Lin-lang Mi-shih Ts'ung-shu,* second series; Reprint. *PP* 65/2.

Liu, James, J. Y. *Major Lyricists of the Northern Sung: A.D. 960–1126.* Princeton: Princeton University Press, 1974.

―――. "Some Literary Qualities of the Lyric (*Tz'u*)." In *Studies in Chinese Literary Genres,* ed. Cyril Birch, pp. 133–53. Berkeley and Los Angeles: University of California Press, 1974.

Liu Tao-ch'un 劉道醇 . *Wu-tai Ming-hua Pu-yi* [A Supplement to "Great Painters of the Five Dynasties"]. Reprint. *Ssu-k'u Ch'üan-shu Chen-pen,* fifth series, Vol. 230.

Liu Wu-chi, and Irving Yucheng Lo, eds., *Sunflower Splendor: Three Thousand Years of Chinese Poetry.* Garden City: Anchor Books, 1975.

Liu Yi-ch'ing 劉義慶 . *Yu-ming Lu* [Records of the Obscure and the Visible]. *Lin-lang Mi-shih Ts'ung-shu,* third series; Reprint. *PP* 65/3.

Liu Yün-hsiang 劉雲翔 . "Wu-ko yü Tz'u" [Southern Songs and Lyric Poetry]. *T'ung-sheng Yüeh-k'an* 2 (1943?): 119–34 (see Glen Baxter, "Metrical Origins," p. 112 [reprint p. 190], n. 12, for a reference to an earlier publication of this article).

Lu Yu 陸游 . *Nan-T'ang Shu* [History of the Southern T'ang]. Reprint. *Ssu-pu Ts'ung-k'an Hsü-pien.*

Ma Ling 馬令 . *Nan-T'ang Shu* [History of the Southern T'ang]. Reprint. *Ssu-pu Ts'ung-k'an Hsü-pien.*

McNaughton, William, and Lenore Mayhew. *A Gold Orchid.* Tokyo and Rutland: Tuttle, 1972.

Marney, John. *Liang Chien-wen Ti.* Boston: Twayne Publishers, 1976.

Mizuhara Ikō 水原渭江 . "Nan-Tō Goshu Shi no Kenkyū" [Studies on the Lyric Poems of Li Yü]. Pt. 1, *Otani Jōshi Daigaku Kiyō* vol. 12, no. 1 (1977): 16–33; pt. 2, ibid., vol. 12, no. 2 (1978): 30–71.

Murakami Tetsumi. "Gyofu Shi Kō" [A Study of "Old Fisherman" Lyrics]. *(Shūkan) Tōyōgaku* 18 (1967): 39–50.

―――. "'Shokuhai,' 'Teihai' to iu Koto: Dokushi Saki" [Stray Notes from Reading Lyric Poetry—the Case of "Candle Put Aside" and "Lamp Put Aside"]. *Chūgoku Bungaku Hō* 1 (1954): 86–92.

Naba Toshisada 那波利貞 . "Kankaseraretaru Nan-Tō Bunka no Kachi" [The Overlooked Value of Southern T'ang Culture]. *Rekishi to Chiri* vol. 4, no. 2 (1919): 21–32; no. 3, 19–32.

Naka Michiyo 双珂通世 . "Shina Fujin Tensoku no Kigen" [The Origin of the Footbinding of Chinese Women]. *Shigaku Zasshi* 9 (1898): 496–520.

Nan Shih [A History of the Southern Dynasties]. Comp. Li Yen-shou 李延壽 et al. Peking: Chung-hua Shu-chü, 1975.

Nienhauser, William H. Jr., *P'i Jih-hsiu.* Boston: Twayne Publishers, 1979.

Obi Kōichi 小尾郊一 . "Nan-Tō no Shi to Shizen" [The Lyric Poems of Southern T'ang and Nature]. *Bukogawa Kokubun* 14–15 (1979): 152–59; Reprint. *Chūgoku Kankei Ronsetsu Shiryō* vol. 21, pt. 2A: 266–69.

Owen, Stephen. *The Poetry of the Early T'ang.* New Haven and London: Yale University Press, 1977.

Pai P'u 白樸 . *T'ien-lai Chi* [The "Piping of Heaven" Collection]. *Chiu Chin-jen Chi*; Reprint. Taipei: Ch'eng-wen Ch'u-pan-she, 1967.

Peterson, Charles A. "The Restoration Completed: Emperor Hsien-tsung and the Provinces." *PT*, 151–91.

Pulleyblank, Edwin G. *The Background of the Rebellion of An Lu-shan*, London Oriental Series, vol. 4. London: Oxford University Press, 1955.

———. "Late Middle Chinese." *Asia Major* 15 (1969): 197–239; 16 (1971): 121–68.

Shao Po 邵博 . *Ho-nan Shao Shih Wen-chien Hou-lu* [Later Records of Things Seen and Heard by Mr. Shao of Ho-nan]. *Hsüeh-chin T'ao-yuan*, eighteenth series; Reprint. *PP* 46/24.

Shen Chien-shih 沈兼士 *Kuang yün Sheng-hsi* [The Phonology of the "Kuang-yün"]. 1945? Reprint. Taipei: T'ai-wan Chung-hua Shu-chü, 1969.

Soper, Alexander Coburn. *Kuo Jo-hsü's Experiences in Painting (T'u-hua Chien-wen Chih): An Eleventh Century History of Chinese Painting Together with the Chinese Text in Facsimile*, American Council of Learned Societies Studies in Chinese and Related Civilisations, no. 6. Washington, 1951.

Ssu-k'u Ch'üan-shu Tsung-mu T'i-yao [Essential Notes on (Works Listed in) the Table of Contents of the Complete Collection of the Four Libraries]. Comp. Chi Yün 紀筠 et al. Taipei: T'ai-wan Shang-wu Yin-shu-kuan, 1971.

Sung Shih [A History of the Sung Dynasty]. Comp. T'o-t'o 脫脫 et al. Peking: Chung-hua Shu-chü, 1977.

T'ai-p'ing Yü-lan [Imperial Conspectus of the T'ai-p'ing Era]. Comp. Li Fang 李昉 et al. Reprint. Taipei: T'ai-wan Shang-wu Yin-shu-kuan, 1975.

Takeuchi Teruo 竹內照夫 . "Nan-Tō Chūshu 'Kankeisha' Dainishu no 'Sai'u mukai keisoku en' no Kui ni Tsuite" [On the Meaning of the Line "In fine rain my dreams return to far away Chi-sai" in the Second of Li Ching's Two Lyrics to the Melody "Huan Hsi Sha"]. *Kansai Daigaku*

Chūgoku Bungakkai Kiyō 3 (1970): 41–46 (there is a Chinese translation by Chang Liang-tse 張仄澤 , *Ta-lu Tsa-chih* 40 [1970]: 169–70).

―――. "Nan-Tō Chūshu no Shiku ni Tsuite (saisetsu)" [On a Line by Li Ching—a Further Comment]. *Tōkyō Shinagakuhō* 16 (1972): 49–53.

T'ang Kuei-chang. "Nan-T'ang Yi-wen Chih" [A Bibliography of Works Written in Southern T'ang]. *Chung-hua Wen-shih Lun-ts'ung* 11 (1979): 337–56.

T'ao Tsung-yi 陶宗儀 . *Ch'o-keng Lu* [Notes While Resting from the Plough]. *Chin-tai Mi-shu*, ninth series; Reprint. *PP* 22/4.

Tung Shih 董史 . *Huang Sung Shu-lu* [A Record of Calligraphy from (our) Sung Dynasty]. *Chih-pu-tsu Chai Ts'ung-shu*, sixteenth series; Reprint. *PP* 29/15.

Twitchett, Denis. "The Composition of the T'ang Ruling Class: New Evidence from Tun-huang." *PT*, 47–85.

―――. "Varied Patterns of Provincial Autonomy in the T'ang Dynasty." In *Essays in T'ang Society: The Interplay of Social, Political, and Economic Forces*, ed. John Curtis Perry and Bardwell L. Smith, pp. 90–109. Leiden: E. J. Brill, 1976.

―――, and Arthur F. Wright. "Introduction." *PT*, 1–43.

Waley, Arthur. "A Chinese Poet in Central Asia." In *The Secret History of the Mongols and Other Pieces*, pp. 30–46. London: Allen and Unwin, 1963.

―――. *Yuan Mei: Eighteenth Century Chinese Poet*. London: Allen and Unwin, 1956.

Walls, Jan W. "The Poetry of Yü Hsüan-chi: A Translation, Annotation, Commentary, and Critique." Ph.D. Dissertation, University of Indiana, 1972.

Wang Chi 王績 . *Tung-kao-tzu Chi* [The Works of the Master of the Eastern Meadow]. Reprint. *Ssu-pu Ts'ung-k'an Hsü-pien*.

Wang Chih 王銍 . *Mo Chi* [Memories]. Shanghai: Shang-wu Yin-shu-kuan, 1919.

Wang Gungwu. "The Middle Yangtse in T'ang Politics." *PT*, 193–235.

―――. *The Structure of Power in North China During the Five Dynasties*. Stanford: Stanford University Press, 1967.

Wang Kuo-wei 王國維 . "Nan-T'ang Erh-chu Tz'u Pu-yi" [A Supplement to the "Lyric Poems of the Two Lords of the Southern T'ang"], *T'ang Wu-tai Erh-shih-yi Chia Tz'u-chi* [Collected Lyric Poems of Twenty-one T'ang and Five Dynasties Writers]. *Wang Kuan-t'ang Hsien-sheng Chi* [Collected Works of Mr. Wang Kuo-wei], vol. 15. Taipei: Wen-hua Ch'u-pan Kung-ssu, 1968.

Wang Wei 王維 . *Wang Yu-ch'eng Chi Chien-chu* [Annotated Works of Wang Wei], annot. Chao Tien-ch'eng 趙殿成 . Hong Kong: Chung-hua Shu-chü, 1972.

Wen Hsüan [Literary Selections]. Comp. Hsiao T'ung 蕭統 . Reprint. Taipei: Cheng-chung Shu-chü, 1971.

Wen Yi-to 聞一多 . "Ts'en Chia-chou Hsi-nien K'ao-cheng" [An Examination of the Chronology of Ts'en Shen]. In *T'ang Shih Tsa-lun* [Miscellaneous Discussions of T'ang Poetry], pp. 101–42. Peking: Ku-chi Ch'u-pan-she, 1956.

Wen-ying 文瑩 . *Yü-hu Ch'ing-hua* [Pure Remarks from a Jade Pot]. *Chih-pu-tsu Chai Ts'ung-shu*, sixth series; Reprint. *PP* 29/6.

Wimsatt, Genevieve. *Selling Wilted Peonies: Biography and Songs of Yü Hsüan-chi, T'ang Poetess*. New York: Columbia University Press, 1936.

Workman, Michael E. "The Bedchamber *Topos* in the *Tz'u* Songs of Three Medieval Chinese Poets: Wen T'ing-yün, Wei Chuang, and Li Yü." In *Critical Essays in Chinese Literature*, ed. William H. Nienhauser Jr., et al., pp. 167–86. Hong Kong: The Chinese University, 1976.

Wu-kuo Ku-shih [Stories of the Five States]. *Chih-pu-tsu Chai Ts'ung-shu*, eleventh series; Reprint. *PP* 29/10.

Yang Shen 楊慎 . *Tz'u-p'in* [The Grades of Lyric Poetry]. *Tz'u-hua Ts'ung-pien*; Reprint. Taipei: Kuang-wen Shu-chü, 1970.

Yeh Ting-yi 葉鼎彝 . "T'ang Wu-tai Tz'u Lüeh-shu" [A Brief Account of Lyric Poetry in the T'ang and Five Dynasties]. *Shih-ta Yüeh-k'an* 22 (1935): 130–47; 23 (1936): 110–30.

Yu Kuo-en 游國恩 . "Lüeh-t'an Li Hou-chu Tz'u ti Jen-min-hsing" [Briefly Remarking on the Popular Character of Li Yü's Lyric Poems]. In *Li Yü Tz'u T'ao-lun Chi* (see above, section A.3), pp. 62–72.

Yu Mou 尤袤 . *Sui-ch'u T'ang Shu-mu* [A List of Writings in the Hall of Accord with my Original (Purpose)]. *Hai-shan Hsien-kuan Ts'ung-shu*; Reprint. *PP* 60/1.

Yü Chia-hsi 余嘉錫 . *Ssu-k'u T'i-yao Pien-cheng* [A Critical Examination of the Essential Notes on the Four Libraries]. Taipei: Yi-wen Yin-shu-kuan, 1965.

Yuan Chiung 袁褧 , and Yuan Yi 頤 . *Feng-ch'uang Hsiao-tu* [Brief Jottings by a Maple Tree Window]. *Pao-yen T'ang Mi-chi*; Reprint. *PP* 18/14.

Yuan Mei 袁枚 . *Tzu-pu-yü* [What Confucius Didn't Say]. *Pi-chi Hsiao-shuo Ta-kuan Hsü-pien*; Reprint. Taipei: Hsin-hsing Shu-chü, 1962.

Yuan Wen 袁文 . *Weng-yu Hsien-p'ing* [Idle Comments from a Jar-mouth Window]. *Wu-ying Tien Chü-chen-pan Shu*; Reprint. *PP* 27/41.

C. OTHER WORKS CONSULTED

Altieri, Daniel P. "The Role of the Yu-fu in Early Chinese Literature: A Study of the Yu-fu of Li Yü and Chang Chih-ho with Original Translations from the Classical Chinese." *Tamkang Review* vol. 3, no. 2 (1972): 129–39.

Aoyama Hiroshi. "Ri Iku no Shoki no Shi Sanshu" [Three Lyric Poems from Li Yü's Early Period]. *Kangaku Kenkyū, Bukkan* 2 (1964): 1–13.

Carpenter, Bruce E. "Problems of Style in the *Tz'u* Poetry of Wei Chuang." *Tezukayama Daigaku Kiyō* 12 (1975): 25–51.

Chang Wan 張婉 . "P'u-sa Man chi Ch'i Hsiang-kuan chih Chu Wen-t'i" [(The Melody) "P'u-sa Man" and Problems Related to It]. *Ta-lu Tsa-chih* vol. 20, no. 1 (1950): 19–24; no. 2: 15–17; no. 3: 27–32.

Chu Chin-chiang 朱錦江 . "Lüeh-lun Nan-T'ang Erh-ling Wen-wu" [A Brief Discussion of Cultural Objects from the Two Southern T'ang Tombs]. *Hsin Chung-hua Pan-yüeh-k'an* vol. 14, no. 12 (1951): 34–35.

Chuang Yen 莊嚴 . "Li Yü." In *Chung-kuo Wen-hsüeh Shih Lun-chi* [Collected Discussions on the History of Chinese Literature], ed. Chang Ch'i-yün 張其昀 , vol. 2, pp. 491–505. Taipei: Chung-hua Wen-hua Ch'u-pan Shih-yeh-she, 1958.

Chung-kuo Wen-hsüeh Shih [A History of Chinese Literature]. Comp. Literary Research Institute of the Chinese Academy of Sciences. Peking: Jen-min Wen-hsüeh Ch'u-pan-she, 1962.

Han Ming-t'ung 韓名銅 . "Nan-T'ang ti Hsiao-Chou Hou" [The Younger Chou Empress of Southern T'ang]. *Ch'ang-liu* vol. 9, no. 3 (1954): 3–4.

Han Shu-wen 韓書文 . "Tu Li Hou-chu Tz'u Shu-hou" [Written After Reading the Lyric Poems of Li Yü. *Chien-she Chi-k'an* 1 (1931): 70 73.

Ho Yung-jen, 何勇仁 "Nan-T'ang Li Yü: Ch'i Jen Ch'i Yi" [Li Yü of Southern T'ang—the Man and His Art]. *Hsin T'ien-ti* vol. 5, no. 3 (1966): 23–25.

Hsieh Shih-ya. "Li Yü Tz'u Yen-chiu" [A Study of the Lyric Poems of Li Yü]. *Nan-ta Chung-wen Hsüeh-pao* 1 (1962): 1 12.

Hu P'in-ch'ing 胡品清 . "Lun Li Hou'chu ti Tz'u" [On the Lyric Poems of Li Yü]. *Wen-t'an* 70 (1966): 9 11. Reprint. *Meng-huan Tsu-ch'ü* [A Suite of Dreams], pp. 175–88. Taipei: Shui-niu Ch'u-pan-she, 1967.

Hu Pin-ching." Appreciation of Li Hou-chu's Poems, Later Period." *Chinese Culture* vol. 13, no. 3 (1972): 67–77.

———. "Ten Poems by Li Hou-chu, the King Poet." *Chinese Culture* vol. 6, no. 3 (1965): 87–92.

———. "The Poetical Works of Li Hou-chu." *Chinese Culture* vol. 13, no. 1 (1972): 97–112.

Hu Yün-yi　胡雲翼　. *Li Hou-chu Tz'u* [The Lyric Poems of Li Yü]. Hong Kong: T'ai-p'ing-yang T'u-shu Kung-ssu, n.d.

Jao Tsung-yi　饒宗頤　. *Tz'u-chi K'ao* [An Examination of Textual Sources for Lyric Poems]. Hong Kong: Hong Kong University Press, 1963.

Li Chin-lin　黎淦林　. "Li Hou-chu ti Lian-ai Sheng-huo" [The Love Life of Li Yü]. *Wen-hsüeh Shih-chieh* 42 (1964): 43–49.

Li Ta-fang　李大防　. "Tu Li Hou-chu Tz'u Shu-hou" [Written After Reading Li Yü's Lyric Poems]. *Wen-shih Ts'ung-k'an* 1 (1935): 41–42.

Lin Lin　林林　. "Li Yü ti Chiao-hsün" [The Warning Example of Li Yü]. *Shih-ko Tsa-lun* [Miscellaneous Discussions of Poetry], pp. 119–23. Hong Kong: Jen-chien Shu-wu, 1949.

Liu Cheng-hao　劉正浩　. "Nan-T'ang Li Hou-chu Lun" [A Discussion of Li Yü of Southern T'ang], pt. 1. *Hai-feng* 3 (1958): 13–17.

Lu K'an-ju　陸侃如　, and Feng Yuan-chün　馮沅君　. *Chung-kuo Shih Shih* [A History of Chinese Poetry]. Reprint. Hong Kong: Ku-wen Shu-chü, 1968.

Lu K'an-lu　陸衍盧　. "Tz'u-jen Li Hou-chu" [The Lyric Poet Li Yü]. 2:1–20.

Lu Tai-tseng　盧逮曾　. "Wu-tai Chün-chu ti Wen-hsüeh" [The Literature of Rulers During the Five Dynasties], pt. 2. *Chung-fa Ta-hsüeh Yüeh-k'an* 2 (1932): 43–59 (a slightly revised version of the section discussing Li Yü is reprinted as "Lun Nan-T'ang Hou-chu ti Wen-hsüeh" [A Discussion of the Literature of Li Yü of Southern T'ang], *Min-chu Hsien-cheng* vol. 5, no. 7 [1953]: 17–19).

Lung Mu-hsün　龍沐勛　. "*Nan-T'ang Erh-chu Tz'u* Hsü-lun" [A Prefatory Discussion of the "Lyric Poems of the Two Lords of Southern T'ang"]. *LHTT*, 1:1–11.

Nan-T'ang Erh-ling Fa-chüeh Pao-kao [A Report on the Excavation of Two Southern T'ang Tombs]. Comp. Nanking Museum (Nan-ching Po-wu-kuan). Peking: Wen-wu Ch'u-pan-she, 1957.

Pan Shu-ko　班書閣　. "*Nan-T'ang Shu* Chien-chu Yin-shu piao" [Table of Works Quoted in the Annotations to the "History of Southern T'ang"]. *Kuo-li Pei-p'ing T'u-shu-kuan Kuan-k'an* vol. 9, no. 4 (1935): 9–20.

She Hsüeh-man　佘雪曼　. *Li Hou-chu Tz'u Hsin-shang* [An Appreciation of Li Yü's Lyric Poems]. Hong Kong: Wen-ying Ch'u-pan-she. [1953?].

Su Shih　蘇軾　(attrib.). *Tung-p'o Chih-lin* [Su Shih's Grove of Stories]. *Pai-ch'uan Hsüeh-hai*; Reprint. *PP* 2/3.

Sung Tzu-pao　宋慈抱　. "*Nan-T'ang Shu Pu-chu* Hsü" [Preface to "Supplementary Annotations to the History of Southern T'ang"]. *Ou-feng Tsa-chih* 1 (1934): 6a–7b.

BIBLIOGRAPHY

T'ang Wen-te 唐文德 . *Li Hou-chu Tz'u Ch'uang-tso Yi-shu ti Yen-chiu* [A Study of the Art of Creation in Li Yü's Lyric Poems]. T'ai-chung: Kuang-ch'i Ch'u-pan-she, 1975.

Tao-shan Ch'ing-hua [Pure Talks from the Mountain of the Way]. *Pai-ch'uan Hsüeh-hai*; Reprint. *PP* 2/10.

Tiao-chi Li-t'an [Chats While Standing on the Fishing Terrace]. Comp. Shih —— ——. *Chih-pu-tsu Chai Ts'ung-shu*, fourth series; Reprint. *PP* 29/4.

Twitchett, Denis. "Provincial Autonomy and Central Finance in Late T'ang." *Asia Major* 11 (1964): 211–32.

Wei Chin-man 韋金滿 . "Li Hou-chu Tz'u Hsin-shang" [An Appreciation of Li Yü's Lyric Poems]. *Hsin-ya Hsüeh-yuan Chung-kuo Wen-hsüeh-hsi Nien-k'an* 4 (1966): 66–73.

Wixted, John Timothy. *The Song-Poetry of Wei Chuang (836–910 A.D.)*, Arizona State University Centre for Asian Studies Occasional Paper No. 12. Tempe, 1979.

Wu Shu 伍 淑. "Nan-T'ang Chung-chu ho T'a ti Tz'u" [Li Ching and His Lyric Poems]. *Ch'ang-liu* vol. 33, no. 4 (1966): 17–18.

Yang Hsien-yi 楊憲益 . "Li Pai yü P'u-sa Man" [Li Po and (the Melody) "P'u-sa Man"], *Ling-mo Hsin-chien* [New Notes in Faded Ink], pp. 1–8. Shanghai: Chung-hua Shu-chü, 1947.

Yeh Te-jung 葉德容 . "Wang-kuo Tz'u-jen Li Hou-chu Lun" [A Discussion of Li Yü, the Lyric Poet Who Lost his Kingdom]. *Hsia-ta Chou-k'an* 12–13 (1935): 15–19.

Yü Pi-yün 俞陛雲 . "*Nan-T'ang Erh-chu Tz'u* Chi-shu" [An Account of the "Lyric Poems of the Two Lords of Southern T'ang"]. *T'ung-sheng Yüeh-k'an* vol. 1, no. 10 (1943): 55–64; no. 11: 37–47.

Yü-wo 余 我. "Wan-ching Ch'i-liang Liang Tz'u-jen" [Two Lyric Poets of Evening Chill]. *Ch'ien-t'an Chi* [Shallow Remarks], pp. 32–35. Taipei: Shui-niu Ch'u-pan-she, 1968.

INDEX

An Lu-shan Rebellion (755–763), xvi

Baxter, Glen (contemporary scholar), lvi
Beethoven, Ludwig van (1770–1827), xl
Boudoir lament (style of poetry), xxxii

Chan An-t'ai (editor of Li Ching and Li Yü), 79
Ch'ang-an (T'ang capital), xxxv, xxxviii, 53, 125
Chang Yi-fang (Southern T'ang official), 107
Chao-hui (Empress), 89
　death of, xxiv–xxv
　Li Yü's dirge for, xxiv–xxv, xlvii, 114–21
　marriage to Li Yü, xxiii
Chao-yang Palace (Han dynasty), xxxviii, 19, 24, 27
Ch'en P'eng-nien (961–1017, Sung philologist), xxii, 123
Chen Shih-chuan (contemporary scholar), lvi
Ch'en T'ao (poet), lvii
Ch'en Yin-k'o (historian), lvi
Ch'eng-ti (Han dynasty emperor, reg. 32–6 B.C.), xxxviii
Ch'i-chiu Hsü-wen (Ch'en Hu), 69
Chi-sai ("Cock Fort"), 64
Chiang-ling (capital of Liang dynasty), 110
Chiang-piao Chih (historical work on Southern T'ang), 123
Ch'in-huai (stream in Nanking), 86
Chin-ling (Nanking), 33
Chin-lou-tzu (Hsiao Yi), 110
Ching-chou (Chiang-ling), 110
Ch'ing-ming (spring holiday), xxxvii, 15–16, 25, 75
Ch'ing-nu (Southern T'ang palace maid), 102
Ch'o-keng Lu (T'ao Tsung-yi), liv–lv
Chou Chao-hui, see Chao-hui (Empress)
Chou Wen-chü (Southern T'ang figure painter), xxiii
Chü-jan (tenth century landscape painter), xxii–xxiii
Chüan-tzu (Methuselah figure), 124
Cold Food (spring holiday), xxxvii, 13
Confucius, 116

Dirge (lei), literary form, 125
Double Nine (autumn holiday), xxxvii, 97
Dreaming Jewel, 56
Drunken Land, 66

Empress Chao-hui. See Chao-hui (Empress)
Empress Wu (T'ang dynasty, reg. 684–705), xxxiv
Examination system, role in emergence of literati, xxxiv

Fang Hui (1227–1306, Yuan dynasty critic and anthologist), xlvi, 124
Feng-ch'uang Hsiao-tu (Yuan Chiung and Yuan Yi), 124
Feng Yen-chi (mistake for Yen-ssu), liii
Feng Yen-ssu (903–960), xv
　character of, xix–xxii
　life of, xxii
　prose writings, xlv
　shih poetry, xlv, xlvii, 107
　tz'u poetry, xix, xxi, xxx, xl–xli, xliii, xlv–xlvi
　　"Ch'üeh T'a Chih" (2), xli
　　"Ch'üeh T'a Chih" (10), xlii
　　"Ch'üeh T'a Chih" (13), xlii–xliv
　　collection of, xlv
　　"Huan Hsi Sha," 131
　　in history of genre, xlv
　　problems of authenticity, xlvi, 85
　　"Ts'ai Sang-tzu" (2), xlii
　　"Ts'ai Sang-tzu" (6), xliii
　　"Ts'ai Sang-tzu" (7), xli
　　"Yeh Chin Men" (4), xli
Flying Swallow (Chao Fei-yen, consort of Han Ch'eng-ti), xxxviii
Footbinding, association of Li Yü with, xxvi
Frankel, Hans (contemporary scholar), lvii
Fukumoto Masakazu (Japanese scholar), 64

Green Gate (of Ch'ang-an), 53

Han Yü (768–824, T'ang Confucian writer), xxxiv

INDEX